Miracles Do Happen
A walk in the Mystical Lane

Also by the same author

Aruna Jethwani has to her credit three novels, two poetry books, two self-help books, one compilation of short stories titled *The Bridge*, and a biography of Dada J. P. Vaswani. Her translation works from Sindhi into English include Sadhu T. L. Vaswani's autobiography titled *Ecstasy and Experiences: A Mystical Journey*, and a selection of Shah Abdul Latif's poetry titled *The Sufi: Shah Abdul Latif*.

Aruna Jethwani's debut novel *Another Love, Another Sky* was awarded the first prize in the English category by the Authors' Guild of India in 2005. Her Short Story "Bridge on river Krishna" won the first prize in the Rajaji Award competition held in 1991. Her 16 short stories are translated and complied into Marathi under the title *Suneri Gurte, Chanderi Akash*.

Her novel *At the wedding - a tale of Roots…Romance…Prophecy* is of significance to the Sindhi community and is well received all over the world.

Miracles Do Happen
A walk in the Mystical Lane

Aruna Jethwani

STERLING PUBLISHERS (P) LTD.
Regd. Office: A1/256 Safdarjung Enclave,
New Delhi-110029. CIN: U22110DL1964PTC211907
Tel: 26387070, 26386209; Fax: 91-11-26383788
E-mail: mail@sterlingpublishers.com
www.sterlingpublishers.com

Miracles Do Happen: A walk in the Mystical Lane
© 2017, Aruna Jethwani
ISBN 978 81 207 9496 2

All rights are reserved.
No part of this publication may be reproduced, stored in a retrieval system or transmitted, in any form or by any means, mechanical, photocopying, recording or otherwise, without prior written permission of the original publisher.

Printed in India

Printed and Published by Sterling Publishers Pvt. Ltd.,
Plot No. 13, Ecotech-III, Greater Noida - 201306,
Uttar Pradesh, India

Dedicated with love

*to all those who touched
my life and made it beautiful*

Gratitude

To Dada J. P. Vaswani for writing the Foreword;

To Swami Krishnanand (Bhadran) for sharing his personal experiences;

To Dr. Arjun Batra for sharing his precious spiritual mystical books;

To Dr. Sumit Paul for encouraging me to write the book;

To Dr. Arjun Thimmaiah for guiding me through the energy fields;

To Captain Rajeev, Dr. Shirin Venkat, Kamala, Pritam Dada, for being part of my venture;

Many thanks to Rani Motwani for typing the zero draft.

Special thanks to Kamal Thadani for arranging the scattered matter into an appealing book;

To my husband, Arjan, and my daughter, Anjali Kishore Moorjani, for holding my hand, always;

I would be failing in my duty if I don't acknowledge my publisher, S. K. Ghai, of Sterling Publishers and also my editor, Sanjiv Sarin, who gave me invaluable suggestions at every stage of revision of the book.

Foreword

"Do you believe in miracles?" I was asked. And I said, "Life itself is a miracle." A seed becomes a huge banyan tree. A caterpillar becomes a butterfly. A tiny baby becomes a giant of a man. All around us are miracles.

Man himself is a miracle of Nature. There are no two leaves, no two faces of men, animals, birds or insects that are identical in all respects. This is a miracle, although everything living and non-living is made of the same stuff—nuclei and electrons and protons vibrating with each other at different frequencies.

We live in an ever expanding universe. Everything is multiplying. Yet the divine spark (atman) within every one of us and in every thing, remains exclusively unique for every individual. Is this not a miracle of the highest order?

Mrs. Aruna Jethwani, a former Principal of St. Mira's College for girls, is a gifted poet and artist. She has the mind of a scholar and the heart of a child. Her love, kindness, generosity and strength of faith have inspired many and drawn them closer to the Lotus Feet of the Lord. Blessed with the power of intuitive insight and perception, sensitive to the psychic, she has written this book, *Miracles Happen*, which will open a new world to many seekers of Truth.

The word miracle is derived from the Latin miraculum, which means an object of wonder. Blessed is the man, who though having grown in years, yet retains the sense of wonder, which makes every child, childlike.

Many of us are struggling today to comprehend our life, the purpose of our life, life beyond life and, especially, God's plan for our life. I have always felt that we are making an error of judgment in trying to understand things of the spirit with the help of the mind. Even as the ears cannot see and the eyes cannot hear, so the mind cannot explain things of the spirit. There is an inner, mystical, psycho-spiritual dimension, a special level of consciousness, within every one of us, which we must touch through the practise of certain sadhanas.

The quest for the mystical takes us to direct communion with the Unseen, the Eternal. Long ago, when one of the great Sufi Masters, Bayazid, came to Sind in search of enlightenment, he met a mystic named Abu Ali, who gave him three dictums by which to live his life:

1. God is One, by whatever name people may call Him.
2. The One resides in all of His Creation.
3. Annihilate your ego; annihilate yourself. And behold the vision of the Lord!

In these three precepts we have the essence of the mystical path that the Sufi saints walked.

This book makes fascinating reading for everyone looking for some knowledge that is not colloquial or literary. It has not been written out of imagination, but has been garnished with testified happenings and genuine places, which are of interest to the subject. Several aspects of mysticism have been touched.

The mystical awareness is essentially one of internal experience. It is, indeed, commendable that Mrs. Jethwani has managed to capture it in words! I am sure her book will awaken many readers to the call of the Higher Consciousness that is present in each one of us.

J. P. VASWANI

Janamashtami, 2016
Sadhu Vaswani Mission,
10, Sadhu Vaswani Path,
Pune 411001

Contents

	Gratitude	6
	Foreword	7
1.	**Everyone Loves a Miracle**	**13**
	A Window to My Thoughts!	14
2.	**Glimpses of the Mystical Lane**	**17**
	The Mystical Lane	18
	The Little Door	19
	Over a Cup of Coffee	19
	Stuck in a Lift	20
	A Corporate Medium	21
	The Tarot Card Reader	22
	Walk Up the Mystical Lane	23
	The Midnight Rendezvous	24
3.	**Mystical Hills**	**27**
	The Location of Miracles	28
	Real Experiences on Mystical Hills	32
	Miracle of Sabarimala Hills	33
	Girnar Hills: Medallion of Miracles	38
	Shiva Power: A Temple in the Forest	39
	Lay Person's Experience: The Invisible Man	41
	The Mystical Woman	42
	Yogini Devi Seen in Physical Form	43

4.	**Your Dreams Are My Dreams**	**49**
	Our Dreams	50
	When Dreams Come True	51
	The Painting Flew from Mt. Fuji in Japan to Dubai	51
	Kamala's Story: Chhota Hemkunt	55
	Gurudwara Chhota Hemkunt Sahib Begampura (Maharashtra)	56
	Other Temples Built through Dreams	61
5.	**Mystical Dreams**	**63**
	To Dream or Not to Dream	64
	Types of Dreams	64
	Dream Box on My Shelf	66
	Asha's Dream	66
	Rukmani's Dream	66
	Ujwala's Dream	68
6.	**Secrets of Miracles**	**71**
	The Jasmine Flower	72
	Duplicate, Triplicate, and Selfie	74
	Baba Nebhraj: The Mystery of Ether Double	76
7.	**Miracle Tools**	**79**
	Siddhis	80
	Siddhis of Black Magic	80
	Swami Vivekanand's First Fascination	81
	The Siddhi Performer: A Web of Secrets	82
	Getting Out of the Trap: Simple Sadhna	84

Contents   11

Sadhna	84
Meditation	86
Affirmation Prayer	87
Chanting	88
Sadhna and Past Karma	88
Mantra Power Compared to Siddhi Power	89
Occult Powers: Siddhis and Mantras.	90
Secret Yoga Sutras of Patanjali	91
Crystal Songs and Siddhi Stories Narrated by Saints	92
Swami Vivekananda's Views on Siddhis	93
Reading the Unseen	94

8. Mystical Healing   **95**

Mystical Therapy	96
Light Therapy	97
Reiki	98
Healing Rituals	100
Symbol Worship	101

9. Mystical Connect   **103**

Miracles of Connecting	104
Saints and the Dreams	107
A Beautiful Life after Life	107
Miracles or Premonitions: Death Is Light	109
Premonition 1	110
Premonition 2	111
Premonitions of Death	112
Swami Ramakrishna Parmahans	112

Sadhu T. L. Vaswani	113
His Love for His Wife: She Visited Him Every Night	113
The Unseen's True Love	119
True Love Lifts You Up To a Higher Self	121
The Night Vigil	122
They Remember Their Previous Life	123
Rajul, Who Was Gita	123
Mischief Mongers: The Mystery of Roaming Souls	126
Justice Through Reincarnation	131
Story of Dhanpal and Govindsinh	131
Occult Powers of Yogis	135
10. Mystical Experiences	**139**
Sources	*143*

1

Everyone Loves a Miracle

*Maybe a miracle is waiting to happen for you;
You, only you have to find the way!*

A Window to My Thoughts!

We live in thrilling times. We are privileged to know about the power of the Universe and the nature of its working. This helps us to go through various hurdles, adversities and enigmas of life with the minimum of distress and frustration.

There is always invisible help available, provided we are willing to return the same help to others. This help and guidance comes in a variety of ways. It is to be harvested in a particular way. In today's complex life, such help brings comfort and healing.

The Universe is open. There is no need to fear in this open Universe. The law of justice is infinitely active.

It is in the interest of everyone to love and not to hate. Love is the most positive energy in the Universe. It is a good enough reason for it to be the basic law of life. Love is the source of all creation and therefore the highest law of nature.

Someone has said that the Universe is a huge echoing machine. It is much more than that! Standing on the shore, throw a stone in the water. It forms a ripple, which becomes bigger and spreads till it meets the shore where it dissolves. Positive energy is like that. It returns after completing a circle, but after growing bigger and bigger.

The same rule applies to negative thoughts. They will return to you with interest piled high on it. In simple words, if you have deliberately hurt or harmed or hated anyone, the same shall be returned to you with interest.

Mystical experiences are personal and subjective, but one thing is certain — we all are spiritual and mystical beings. And with that super power embedded in the collective human psyche, every miracle is possible.

"A Sindhi, knowingly or unknowingly, is a mystic," wrote William Gibb. By destiny's design, I was born in a Sindhi family. Going by William Gibb's statement, mysticism is in my genes. My curiosity in mystical happenings was stirred in childhood, by the stories told by my grandmother and my mother. While grandmother narrated miracles stories from Guru Nanak's life, my mother, being more intuitive, narrated stories from the life of saints heading the Durbars — the Sindhi Shrines or places of worship. One such story, referring to the double ether, of Baba Nebhraj is narrated in this book.

My curiosity remained dormant till the age of 21 years. The English education, with disdain for deity and ritualistic worship, stopped me from visiting any place of worship, be it a temple, or a church or a dargah. The logical mind questions the basics of all rituals and the hundreds of deities shining on the horizon of Hinduism.

A chance meeting with Late Swami Krishnanandji of Bhadran, an arts graduate and master of as many as nine languages, initiated my curiosity in things mystical. He shared his mystical experiences with us rather generously whenever he visited our home. However, it was my meeting with Sadhu Vaswani, a great scholar, thinker, writer and educationist which made the difference. His simple philosophy of love — the true worship of the divine — captured my heart. But the little door was opened miraculously by the kindness of Dada J. P. Vaswani, the great Sindhi spiritual leader.

It is said that what one receives should be shared, for that is the true purpose of receiving.

2

Glimpse of the Mystical Lane

The Mystical Lane

This book is about psychic power. It is about mystical phenomenon and experiences, objectively recorded and analysed, and explained in a simple manner.

Mystical experiences transcend the presently known theories of science. Mystics are mysterious messengers of God. When they receive His command, they answer the call of the believers. They appear in a dream and give guidance. They increase their ether form to save devotees in trouble. Strange are their ways.

Till recently, mystery surrounded these messengers. Today we know that mystics are intuitive; they are seers who can foresee a catastrophe, they can communicate with the world beyond, and they function beyond time and space. They have experienced the Oneness. They are aware of the Whole from which this entire web of Universe is created.

The Cosmic Universe functions according to the laws which are the Truth and hence cannot be negated and discarded.

This book brings true incidents, providing glimpses of the mystery that surrounds us. It also makes us aware of the mystical splendour, which is truly amazing as it reaffirms the link between the inner and the outer world of humans. It is through the outer world that one can reach the inner world. Though everything is possible at the physical level, it is the Supreme Being who overlooks the inner world of the Spirit. This book has four segments:

1. Mystical Hills, difficult to believe mystical experiences at Girnar hills, Gujarat; Sabarimala; Kerala; and Madhavpur, Gujarat. It also describes the invisible Yogini Devi and the invisible Temple.

2. Mystical Dreams, with stories of dreams coming true, the anatomy of dreams, the carry home messages of dreams and the dream box. It also includes travel of the

sacred painting to Dubai and parallel stories from Sri Ramakrishna and Rabia.
3. Secrets of Miracles and the explanation of Siddhis, with stories of producing a flower from thin air, with the messages here is that mantras are more powerful than Siddhis, that physical world is governed by the physical laws, and the spiritual world is governed by the laws of the spirit.
4. Mystical Connect and the communication with the world beyond, with experiences of lay persons and the communication with the world beyond by well-known saints of India. It also describes reincarnation and mentions that death is a light.

Miracles happen when you are ready to receive them. You will be ready to receive them only when you open the window of your heart. The window will open on the mystical, amazing, and wonderful phenomenon – a little door, giving you a peep into the mystical lane.

The Little Door

Let's get a glimpse . . .
The little door opens when you are at the end of your tether and you seek solutions to numerous problems. Suddenly, your Guardian Angel appears, removing the thorns from your way. Holding you by your little finger, your Guardian Angel leads you to joy, peace, and a beautiful emotion called *love*. And lo! A great miracle has happened, like a drooping bud suddenly blooming and shining to become the centre of attraction; or sun peeping through bare branches of a tree. All this attracts positive energy which helps in wish fulfilment.

Over a Cup of Coffee

This is an interesting incident that happened to me.

> We met over a cup of coffee at a local restaurant. A friend had insisted that I meet him. A bright, radiant face with a sunny

smile, he was there, waiting, before I reached. Apologizing for the few minutes' delay, with a palpitating heart, I sat next to him. As we sipped coffee, we talked of several things, especially about places with higher magnetic fields and the energies of places of pilgrimage, till we started to discuss the concept of time and how some people are gifted with "time sight". Then he took out a piece of paper and explained the linear concept of time.

"Let's begin from this point," he said and wrote something on the paper. Can you guess what he wrote? My birthdate! When I expressed surprise, he smiled and said, "It is there, a benchmark in your life. I can read it!" To many, this may not sound a mystery, especially those who have read of the huge psychic power of Swami Vivekananda. To me it was a door to another world — another intriguing incident to my collection of mystical incidents.

Often, by divine mercy, an angel unlocks the little door, so that you can get a glimpse of the mysterious miracles. Today, mystics are open about the tools and techniques of learning the invisible art. There was a time everything mysterious was unexplained and kept secret. The incidents were considered miracles by common people. Hence Hafz, the Sufi, said centuries ago, "For the enigma to resolve, none ever knew nor yet shall know the truth." Today, things are different. Maybe, the miracles of today will be the science of tomorrow.

Stuck in a Lift

Sometimes you get stuck in a lift and feel suffocated and frustrated. Similar feelings also happen to all ambitious people at some point in their lives. At some step or the other, they are stuck — they cannot move up or cross over the hump. In a car, if you are in neutral gear and you begin to slip back, you change gears. In life, to move up, we choose guides such as astrologers, holy persons, clairvoyants, or even Tarot Card readers.

It was in an uncertain situation when I met Niket. At that time, in the year 2001, every young man and woman went to him for help—whether they were in an IT (Information Technology) company or in love or in college, unable to make the grade—whoever got stuck in a lift, went to him for a solution. I, more out of curiosity than to seek a solution, visited him. I wanted to know why so many young people went to him. What was so special about him? I had just retired from my career, and had time on my hands. I was stuck in my writing profession, and looked for someone to guide me. I decided to follow the line of my young friends; I went to meet him. My first impression of him wearing jeans and T shirt with mobile stuck on his ear was rather mixed. A colleague had accompanied me. She introduced me to him, and we exchanged pleasantries. We chatted for a while; I felt thirsty, and he brought us orange juice, after which he gave the generic advice meant for both of us:

Ask for help and you shall receive it.

I returned half convinced. And forgot all about him.

A Corporate Medium

Sometime in 2003, my computer teacher, Mrs. Patil, talked of an IT fellow, who was keen to help people through his psychic powers. She narrated her friend's case who was relieved of her guilt complex which was the cause of her depression. She talked of his unique and rather unbelievable "past life therapy".

"You must meet him, he guides beautifully," said my computer teacher. "Oh, he is unbelievable! His past life therapy is simply great," she added.

So reluctantly, one morning, she and I went to meet him. He was none other than Niket whom I had met in 2001. This time also I found nothing extraordinary about him. Maybe he could read my mind, but that's a common skill.

It was on my third visit, in 2006 or 2007, when I had gone along with my daughter, that he described my death scene of my immediate past birth. He described it exactly the way the Tarot Card reader had done in 2002. Two different persons, one a Tarot Card reader and the other a Medium assisted by his spiritual guide Meher Baba — two persons belonging to two different communities, divided by time and space (location), totally unconnected, had described my death scene in previous life exactly in the same words, without touching me, without asking my date of birth. I found it amazingly extraordinary.

The Tarot Card Reader

Like every year, the Women Entrepreneurs' exhibition was held at the Blue Diamond hotel in Pune. Having nothing much to do, I wandered around aimlessly, visiting stalls put up by young entrepreneurs, many of them happening to be my students from the college where I taught. I stopped at a sign which said "Rs. 300 for 3 Questions". The sign was hung outside a small black cubicle. Without thinking, I said rather loudly, "Who is going to pay Rs. 300 for 3 questions?" This was in 2002. My loud voice questioning the price charged by the Tarot Card reader reached the person sitting inside.

Immediately, a well-built lady, wearing a long, black Chinese gown, came out. "Ma'am, I will not charge you anything," she said and flashed a sweet smile at me. Seeing my puzzled look, she said, "Ma'am, you are my teacher, so I owe it to you to read the cards free for you." She then gave the details of how she had bunked college for weeks, and had been a free spirit. Perhaps that helped her to develop intuition so necessary in her profession.

Hesitantly, I entered her booth. "Please ask genuine questions. My cards are divine. They always tell the truth."

The truth was that I had no questions to ask. Curiosity is compulsive, so I said rather vaguely, "I have no questions about myself. But I would like to know a thing or two about my daughter." The lady realised that I wasn't genuine in asking my questions. As I was leaving the cabin, she held my hand and looked deep into my eyes, perceiving my aura and reading it. "Ma'am, we never say the things I am about

Glimpse of the Mystical Lane

to tell you. But Ma'am, you have been my teacher and a kind teacher. I am obliged to tell you," she said earnestly.

She then narrated my "death" scene in my immediate past birth. I had no way of believing it, till I met the Medium whose amazing story I have just narrated to you.

How does this knowledge help, you may well ask. Knowing the root cause of your negative self, you will realize that you have to dissolve your past karmas and in that process, move ahead in life without feeling depressed or harbouring ill feelings towards others.

How can the past karmas be dissolved? By doing good karmas, by prayer, by chanting or mantra Jaap, by serving the poor and the needy — in short, by doing kriya or Sadhna of any and every kind.

Walk Up the Mystical Lane

Let's now walk up "The Mystical Lane" and see the splendours of the mysterious phenomena taking place every moment, all around us. The splendour is seen in multi-dimensional colours of the invisible becoming visible, the non-manifest becoming manifest during deep meditation, when human perception is heightened and things which are not seen by the naked eye appear as clear images on the mental horizon.

Modern scientific and technical advancements have solved some of the mysteries of the "invisible" world. One is tempted to believe that the invisible world of yogis, rishis, saints, Pirs, and fakirs has partially become visible, and the so-called miracles are the creation of our own mind.

Electromagnetic photography, which can image the aura and the chakras of the human body, and the recently introduced electro-energy machine, which records the energy and quantifies it, have opened up new vistas of thinking. However, even then there will be mystical happenings beyond the explanation of the existing knowledge. Such flashes or revelations will remain a source of wonder and awe. The mystical splendour will continue to fascinate humankind, perhaps even more with the onset of the New Age, for which the Universe is awaiting eagerly.

This New Age is the age of human awakening, it is the dawn of a new culture of spirituality. The New Age begins where the age of Kalyug ends.

Sadhu T. L. Vaswani wrote in 1950: "Some scientists have begun to talk today of 'Etheric Vision', that is, the power to see in subtler matter — the invisible finer matter — on the astral plane. When Etheric Vision becomes normal, in the days to come, men will know that physical is not the only plane: then will the materialism die."

A lesson, which we must keep revising every day, is that we are a wonderful combination of body, mind, and spirit.

The Midnight Rendezvous

Till recently, mystery surrounded the midnight messengers. Today, we know that mystics are clairvoyant; they are seers who can foresee a catastrophe. They are God's good Samaritans and therefore warn their dear ones of oncoming danger. At midnight, when they meditate, they touch the great cosmic stream of love and compassion and therefore they can immediately sense the vibrations of danger to a devotee.

They can sense the suffering of a human being or the help needed by an individual during times of physical crisis like a tsunami or an earthquake or in times of emotional crisis like a breakdown of a relationship, or loss of a dear one or want of money and the fear of destitution.

Mystics are angels of the night. While the whole world sleeps, angels meditate, they go so much deep within themselves that they become divine sensors. And because of their omnipresent divinity, they know which call to answer and which call to reject.

Mystics are persons of dharma. They are very compassionate. The following is a real incident:

> Years ago, I visited my relatives in Jamnagar to spend my vacation with them. Geeta was one of the family members. She had great desire to meet a saint who was highly educated and scholarly. She expressed this explicitly to me.
>
> Geeta, having been widowed very early in life, was going through a rough patch. By chance she had the darshan of Dada J. P. Vaswani, in Pune. Thereafter, whenever she was in trouble, Dada visited her early morning at 2.30 a.m. She would hear a knock on the entrance door and then see an image of Dada enter her room. His very presence comforted her. The scene would last just a moment.
>
> One afternoon, around 2.30 p.m., she telephoned me. "Dada always visits me during the night. But today, I saw him "real" as I sat down for lunch at 1 o'clock. I do not understand how he came during day time."
>
> I replied, "Geeta, today Dada is in USA. It is early morning over there. Calculate the time at New Jersey. When it is 1 p.m. here, it is exactly 2.30 a.m. there! The saints visit from 12.30 a.m. to 2.30 a.m."

Mystics are messengers of God. When they receive His command, they answer the call of distress. They may appear in a dream and give guidance. They double their ether form to save devotees in trouble. Strange are their ways. They labour during the night. Saints refer to this state as "wakeful in sleep". Dada J. P. Vaswani, on one occasion said, "I walk miles and miles to unknown destinations." Saints live on a higher plane to work for a cosmic cause. They protect us in stormy weather. When good people are in trouble, mystics, in their own secret way, bring them relief. They are not only stress busters but are also saviours who fulfil the higher commands of a Higher Life.

Rumi, the Sufi poet, wrote:

Every night thou freest our spirits from the body,
    And its snare, making them pure like raised tablets,
Every night souls are released from the cages,
    And set free, neither ruling nor ruled.

Jallaludin Rumi

3
Mystical Hills

The Location of Miracles

Have you ever driven uphill without changing gears? No? Then go to Kutch or Saurashtra. Along the white Runn of Kutch of the black hills, there is a short stretch of a hill where you can drive up without changing gears. Recently, while attending the great Kutch festival, we experienced this.

Magnetic Field: Black Hills-Kutch

You may wonder what is so unique about it. There are many sites in the world where, because of high magnetic fields, strange things happen and they are termed as miracles. Interested? Read on!

> The night was dark yet the shadows of trees were visible. There was radiance all around. We sat in the open, on a mountain top, the stars twinkling like a thousand mirrors. The moon was brighter than ever, a pure silver disc lighting the sky. The wind was cold. We shivered as we warmed our hands

over the old Sikkimese *chula* (earthen hearth). Much further down in the valley, the silvery waters of Teesta river flowed peacefully, making the silence of this resort impregnable.

"To talk about mysteries of mystics, we need a quiet place like this," whispered Sakshi.

We had travelled more than a thousand kilometres to reach this beautiful spot. "The place is radiant with beauty. The rishis and the Tibetan monks have touched it and made it sacred. It is only appropriate that we talk of mystical happenings here, and not in the nearby café."

"The place does have powerful vibrations. I can feel them on my skin and in my soul," I replied.

Sakshi gave a little laugh, which rippled down the valley, blown away by the chilling wind.

"Look, look," she suddenly said.

I looked at where she pointed. A white cloud like thing flashed by and disappeared with great speed into the heavens.

"Did you see it?"

"Yes, I did see it." I replied.

"What was it?"

"I don't know."

"What did you see?"

"A white form, tapering at the rear end. It disappeared too soon."

"What do you think? Was it a cloud that evaporated into thin air?"

I tried hard to recollect the form. All I could think was a white form, oblong, around four feet or so long, which was neither a cloud nor a light.

"It was a divine soul. A luminous celestial being, who passed this way to protect us," said Sakshi.

I was mystified. Why would a celestial being visit us? From where had it come and where did it disappear?

Many questions remained unanswered in my mind. At the same time, a wave of joy or maybe peace swept me.

"These beings, the Angelic souls, work ceaselessly for the humankind. They are out there to help people. Help is always available is their message."

I felt like having a hot cup of tea. Putting my shyness aside, I requested for a second and even a third cup of tea. Sakshi was only too happy to share it with me.

"You must be wondering why these luminous beings live here. It is due to the high magnetic field. Mountain peaks have fine energy. In olden days, places of worship were built on mountain or hill tops. There is lot of mythology woven around such places. Miracle stories abound. When people visit these places, their wishes are fulfilled. There is another aspect to it, too. Many yogis and holy men do Yagnya and Tapas there for years, and recharge the vibrations of these places with purity. Purity works miracles."

Sakshi then narrated the common miracle stories abounding in these regions, including the practice of Siddhis by Tapasvis and yogis.

"The known mountain peaks which have powerful magnetic fields are Kedarnath, Girnar Hills, and many other spots in Himalayas, and Western Ghats of India," she informed.

There are many stories of saints, or call them Divine souls, and their psychic powers. Once while visiting Rohtang pass, I felt elevated and emotionally moved by the story of the Saint who lived at the mouth of Beas river, and who attained Samadhi while meditating with his eyes open.

It is there that I wrote:

> The snow bound gorges,
> Guard the Ganga;
> Here the seekers,
> Take an astral walk;
> Have telepathic talk;
> Meditate in meadows,
> Bringing alive shadows.
> Performing mundane miracles;
> The ordinary occult art!
>
> *from Petal on Ganga*

The Indian mythology literature refers to many miracle spots of worship which are charged by high magnetism. The beauty of it is that we, too, can improve our magnetism by doing Kriya or mantra jap.

While Yogis, seekers and saints, leave their vibrations of *tapas* (penance) in their hideouts, there are some locations empowered with alpha vibrations. This could be the reason why every wish made there gets fulfilled. In physical terms,

Old Kedarnath temple

these locations have high magnetic fields.

Outside of Himalayas, there are many hills with mystic power. In western India, the region of Saurashtra and Kutch has locations of "miracles". The area between Porbander and Junagardh has certain power, as in the underground tunnel running between the two cities, which has spiritual vibrations of several divine souls practising tapas. The hills of Girnar have the reputation of being very mystical. In southern India, Sabarimala Hill is equally mystical. Seekers find it easy to meditate and receive divine visions on these hills.

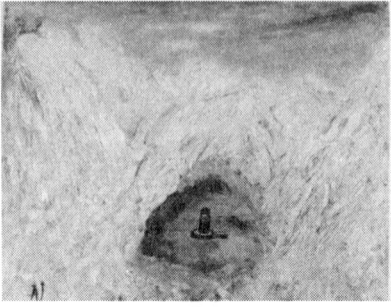

This is an imaginary painting of Shiva Ling in the Himalayas by the author.

Individuals, too, may have their magnetic field. The strength of individual magnetic field can be increased by positive thoughts, deeds, and sounds.

Real Experiences on Mystical Hills

Of the many stories told of the miracles happening, the one that I like the most is narrated by a hard core atheist. Captain Rajeev is a friend living in my neighbourhood. Most of the year he sails on high seas. Sailors have many romantic stories to tell, but Captain Rajeev has many dramatic ones, instead, to share.

One evening, sitting on the terrace of his house, he narrated a frightful encounter with the pirates of the infamous Malacca Straits. Rajeev is an efficient captain, who once steered his ship out of cyclonic storms, a man who is a jolly good fellow, whose reactions to God's miracles are — Are you crazy? Miracles? Mystical? I don't believe this stuff! But that was some time ago.

That day, we prodded him to tell us not about the pirates but about the ghosts on the ships. He smiled. "Ghosts, I have seen none," he said. "Yes, if you want to know about my unexplainable experience at Sabarimala Temple, I am willing to share." Why not? Sabarimala was in the news at that time. The women activists were fighting for their right to enter the temple and break the age old tradition of gender discrimination practised at this most sacred temple in South India.

Miracle of Sabarimala Hills

Rajeev narrated the out of this world phenomenon in great detail. I have summarized and given the basic story.

> There was a long argument at Beena's house. Her husband, Rajeev, refused to listen to her. Beena insisted. He refused. Rajeev was a sea-farer. Like all his colleagues, he lived a happy, carefree life, enjoying a drink with friends and philosophising with colleagues while sailing on the high seas.
>
> In spite of numerous experiences where his life was barely saved, he remained an atheist. He lived by reason and logic rather than religious rituals. On the other hand, Beena believed in their family tradition of certain rituals. Beena had taken a vow that if they were blessed with a child, they would visit Sabarimala. Rajeev did not believe in this kind of promise to God. Of course, sailing on rough seas, sometimes in the eye of a storm, he did feel presence of a supernatural power. But God and visits to temple was not his thing.
>
> "How can you not go? Our eldest son is nine and the youngest is five. This is the appropriate time. You take them to Sabarimala for darshan of our deity," Beena told him.
>
> It was the month of December. Rajeev was home for Christmas holidays. Beena insisted her husband visit Sabarimala at that time for two reasons—their sons were old enough to undertake the arduous journey and 14 January was an auspicious time to visit the Sabarimala temple.

In fact, a supernatural phenomenon takes place on this hill temple at that time. The temple is located on a hilltop, deep inside a forest in Kerala. There are other hills surrounding the temple hill. On every 14 January night, many people have seen a flash of light, which can be seen miles away on other hills, too.

Rajeev was reluctant to go to the Sabarimala temple in the first place. And 14 January night? It was out of question. Millions of devotees throng there to have the vision of the *jyoti* — the flash of light emanating from the precincts of the temple. He would be lost in that mad rush. He feared his children might be hurt or injured in the stampede that happens so often at that time.

So, as a compromise, they decided that he would take the children on 31 December night, instead. It appeared to be a good idea to go on New Year's Eve, when most people would be celebrating New Year at home and there would not be many of them visiting the temple. It would be possible have a good darshan, too.

Rajeev, accompanied by his two children and his brother, planned to reach the junction of river Pumba, which is at the foot of the hill, at around nine o'clock at night. The temple opened at 3.30 a.m. They could conveniently reach the temple by that time as the children would take around six hours to climb the hill.

When they reached Pumba, they were shocked. There were tens of thousands of people, all heading towards the temple, pushing their way up the narrow path on the hill. In fact, there was no place to even get down from the car. Rajeev took the little one, put him on his shoulders and put the bundle of coconuts on his head. Holding his nine-year-old son by his hand and balancing the coconuts carefully, he joined the slowly moving sea of human beings, with his brother following close behind.

Every now and then the devotees had to stop, as the people ahead were slow and there was no room for them to move and climb further. After six hours, Rajeev was around a mile away from the temple.

By that time, all the devotees were exhausted. They lay down by the path to rest and fell asleep, one on top of the other. It was then that Rajeev wanted to turn back and forget about the darshan. He enquired from those beside him if there was a way to go down. "Not really," was the answer. There was only one narrow path to go up, in the front, and one narrow path to go down from behind the temple. Since the hill was so thickly forested, there was no method to find a path to the back of the temple, which would take him down to where the car was parked.

At that stage, Rajeev regretted agreeing to his wife to make the journey for a darshan of the deity. And what a deity! Women were not allowed in the temple. Rajeev did not understand the logic behind the gender discrimination in a temple. He was annoyed with his wife Beena for taking such a silly vow. At that moment, the little fellow on his shoulder said, "I see some people moving through the forest."

"Where?" asked Rajeev.

"There," said his son, pointing a finger in the direction.

"Let's get out of this crowd. Look how they are lying over one another, fast asleep."

The path through the trees was narrow. It did not go down to the bottom of the hill, as Rajeev had thought, but led to a rest house near the temple.

"The rest house must be full. There will be no room for us," said Rajeev loudly to his brother, who was walking very slowly, and taking time to follow him.

But the rest house was empty! The manager was fast asleep, with his head resting on the reception table. Rajeev woke him up. The manager opened his eyes and readily opened the main hall of the rest house for them.

"Let's rest for a while," Rajeev told his children. "There is still an hour for the temple door to open."

Just then there was a knock on the door. A young man, dressed in a white kurta and lungi, stood outside.

"So you wish to have darshan of the Lord? The temple door will open soon. I will take you there."

"Yes," replied Rajeev, surprised to see an unknown man offering to take them to the temple, when tens of thousands of people were waiting at the temple door to rush in as soon as the door opened for a darshan of the deity.

"Give us a few minutes to freshen up," Rajeev requested him.

"Yes," nodded the man and went away.

After a few minutes, he reappeared. He took them through the crowd of hundreds of devotees. Somehow, people just parted and gave them way. They reached the temple just as the door was opening. They were the first ones to be allowed in.

"Would you like to take the priests' blessings?" asked the unknown man.

"Of course!" replied Rajeev.

The man disappeared for a moment.

He reappeared and took them to the Head Priest, who had opened the temple door after doing the *abhishek*. The Head Priest lived a secluded life and did not usually meet devotees. But the unknown man took them through the temple precincts, to the place where the Head Priest lived in a small room.

The Head Priest blessed Rajeev, his brother, and the two children. What an unbelievable thing! They had nothing to offer to the deity or to the Head Priest, as Rajeev had thrown away his bundle of coconuts earlier, out of sheer frustration.

The unknown man then led them back to the rest house. By this time it was four o'clock. The unknown man asked them, "Would you like to carry prasadam for people back at home? Would you like to have breakfast? You all look very hungry."

Within half an hour, the unknown man brought them prasadam. He also bought them hot idlis and dosa and many savouries to eat.

The unknown man gave Rajeev the bill for the food, collected the payment and left. In the excitement of all the happenings, Rajeev realized that he had forgotten to tip the fellow. He rushed and asked the manager, who was still asleep, if he knew anything about the man who had just gone out. But the rest house manager said, "I don't know. I did not see any one come in."

"Not come in, but go out? Who was the man who went out two minutes ago?" Rajeev asked, surprised.

"I didn't see anyone."

Rajeev and his brother ran to the main path, searching for the Good Samaritan. They could not find him. All that they saw was the slowly moving line of human beings, struggling to reach the temple door.

Rajeev stood stunned, for a minute. Who was that man? From where did he come? Where did he vanish? There were no answers. One thing was clear. It was all a mystery and a miracle.

"I believe in the power of Sabarimala Temple and the hills around it. Yes, there is something beyond our rational understanding," Captain Rajeev told us.

The Crystal Chime

The sweet melody you can sing in your heart:

A single miracle can change your life. Rajeev, today is a man of intense faith and believes in the unknown power we call God.

We live in a celestial world where the divine souls are ever ready to help us. They are subtle transformers who, through their mystical powers, give us experiences which are mind-changers.

Sabarimala Temple, Kerala

Girnar Hills: Medallion of Miracles

A little poem narrates it beautifully:
In the forest I sat, smiling,
On the Holy Hills of Girnar.
Listening to whispers of Eternity,
To the vibrations woven into miracles.
The musings of Swamiji,
A purple aura ascends.
In the rhythm of
The Lotus leaves,
The compassion of third eye
Does it all.

The Girnar hills are considered sacred. They an important pilgrimage site for both Jains and Hindus, who gather here during the Girnar Parikrama festival. Girnar hosts a number of temples and some historical spots across its range. Significantly, Girnar hills are popular among Shiva devotees and Gorakhnath yogis for the mystic space-time of the mountain range, with the known presence of many divine souls. Different sects of Sadhus, Babas, and many Jain Tirthankaras visit Girnar during the Maha Shivratri fair.

According to tradition, Pavahari Baba was first initiated into the mysteries of practical yoga on the top of Mount Girnar. Many seekers and aspirants have had beautiful mystical experiences there. Amidst the lush green Gir Forest, the mountain range serves as the hub of religious activity. For Hindus, this place is considered holy as Dattatreya stayed there. The famous Sufi saint and poet Shah Abdul Latif accompanied yogis to the Girnar Hills and was intoxicated by the yogic miracles. There, in his intoxication, he found his Divine Guide. *The Divine Guide makes life easy in today's materialistic age of money power and intense competition.*

Swami Krishnanandji of Bhadran used to visit the Girnar on Shivratri day. On one such occasion he had a mystical experience, beyond time and space. A miracle difficult to believe!

Shiva Power: A Temple in the Forest

"If you want to give in alms, do so on a Shivratri day. Shivratri is very sacred and you will be blessed," said Swamiji. "You may do charity any day or every day, but on auspicious days, it doubles the joy and the blessings." A wonderful philosophy, indeed!

Swamiji was in the habit of going to Girnar every year on Shivratri. On one such occasion, he had a beautiful experience of the power of Shiva. This is how he narrated it:

> It was a Wednesday. Early in the morning, I began to climb the hill since I wished to return by the night and it takes couple of hours of climbing to reach the temple. Thousands of devotees visit the holy shrine situated at the top. On the way to the temple, there are many small places for resting. I had climbed three fourths of the way, when I sat down under a shady tree. Just then a Sadhu came over. He gazed at me and then, pointing to a small opening in the clump of trees, said, "This is an easier way to the shrine. You may take this route to reach up." There was some wisdom in his words and I decided to take that route. "On the way, you will see a Shiva Temple. It is a holy place. You may offer your prayers there before going up," said the Sadhu.

I had barely walked a mile when I came face to face with a stone structure, pyramidal in shape, with a lamp burning inside. I stepped in. There was a Shivling, decorated with vermilion and a few flowers. It was blissful inside the small temple, which looked ancient and yet very bright. I decided to meditate there for a while, before resuming my journey to the hill top.

After a while, I woke up from deep meditation and came out of the temple. To my great surprise, there was no way from there to the temple at the top. I went back the same way I had come. It was already evening by that time and I wondered how I could return to the base by night.

Just then I saw a group of devotees talking of the Dattatreya temple and how it was not crowded since it was a Thursday. The long queue I had seen earlier had almost disappeared. I asked the group, "Today is Wednesday. Why are you talking of today being Thursday?" They laughed and said, "Today is Thursday."

I did not believe them. I saw an old man going through the opening in the jungle, down the small path I had taken earlier as an easy alternative to my destination. I hailed him and asked, "What day is today?" He replied, "It is Thursday." I further queried, "There is a Shiva temple there inside, isn't it?" The man was puzzled. "Shiva temple? I live in that hut down the path. There is no Shiva temple. If you want to visit the Shiva temple, then climb the hill for some time more and you will find the temple. But why did you not come on Shivratri yesterday?"

Shivratri was on Wednesday, and that day was Thursday. It meant I was in meditation for more than twenty four hours! And where was the Shiva temple where I had meditated? It did not exist! And where was the Sadhu who showed me the easy route to this temple?

All these questions remain unsolved. All I can say that there is a great Shiva Power in the Girnar Hills.

The Crystal Wind Chimes

The Bell of Hope

The places of pilgrimages are a mixture of belief and faith. Our ancient rishis could identify the hills, mountain peaks, and underground flows of water which carried the energy and did tapas there. Their tapas helps us even today to get benefit from the highly charged places and get solace and peace, maybe even some help to fulfil our wishes. For miracles to happen, seek the benefits of the tapas done by great saints and seekers.

Mystical Hills all over the world are areas of high magnetic field. They are potent receivers of energy and also generous in giving out energy. The Mystical Hills have a positive impact on humans.

Lay Person's Experience: The Invisible Man

Invisible helpers

A few friends suggested that I could use social media to get to know about true mystical experiences of people living abroad. But very few responded to my posts.

Then I wrote to Dr. Gurubux. Dr. Gurubux is a practising medical doctor in Maryland, Washington, D.C. He was an early immigrant to the USA. He had a mystical streak from childhood itself. He replied to my email immediately. This is his story:

> I have had many mystical experiences, which I am unable to share. But there is one that I would like you to write about. It is about my Guru, a Muslim Pir by the name of Mallik Sahib. He was my father's Guru and also of my father's sister.
>
> My relationship with Mallik Sahib started when Kaka, my father, took us to his Dargah. I was 6 or 7 years old. I have some memories of Ami (Mallik Sahib's wife). Since then, my entire life journey has been guided by Mallik Sahib — my belief and faith. He has been there whenever I needed him.

In 1980, I made my first trip to Rohri, in Pakistan. I was nervous, as I did not know anyone there. Before boarding the plane at Mumbai, there was a Sindhi gentleman from Singapore, standing behind me in the queue. I started talking to him and shared my fear about taxis in Karachi, etc. He assured me that he would stay with me until I got to Sheraton hotel in Karachi, where I would be staying.

After leaving me at the hotel, he gave me his address and agreed to join me for dinner that night. He did not turn up. I never saw him again and was unable to trace him even in Singapore. All my enquiries at his address in Singapore failed, because there was no such addressee, nor the address.

Since that incident and in the process of searching for the invisible man, Mallik Sahib introduced me to a very humble, unselfish, well to do, influential gentleman, who has accompanied me to Rohri on several trips and helped me to build a Dargah.

The Crystal Wind Whispered: Hope

Everyone has a Guardian Angel. There is always help available from the invisible Divine Helpers. Their ways are strange. One has to have faith and call for help from the bottom of the heart. The call is always heard, regardless of the time and space element.

The Mystical Woman

The Beauty Called Yogini Devi

Swami Krishnanadji entered our lives a long time ago. It was curiosity, besides his accented English and a certain undefinable wit, and penchant for punctuality, which drew the family towards him. Among his many mystical stories, which he often narrated to us, the one that really fascinated all of us is of the Yogini Devi, of whom many had talked but none had seen. Except Swamiji.

The memory of Yogini Devi revived recently, when someone told me about a French girl living alone among the shepherds somewhere near Madhavpur, in Saurashtra, and her trips to a nearby hill. She went there to offer worship at the Shiva temple. Could it be the same Shiva temple where Yogini Devi was living? Maybe, maybe not. Let us hear about Yogini Devi from Swamiji, in his own words—his amazing meeting with Yogini Devi, whom no one had met, but many had experienced, whom a few had seen in astral form, but never in a physical body.

Yogini Devi Seen in Physical Form

When people in Adityana village talked to me about Yogini Devi residing atop the nearby hill, I felt excitement surge through me because the information connected with Makarana Sahib's directions to me in a dream. Makarana Sahib was a saint of Sindh who lived a hidden life and worked on the astral plane. As you know, I am a Tamilian born in Burma. During my wanderings in Sindh, I met him in Jacobabad. Later I acknowledged him as my spiritual guide.

People made diverse claims about Yogini Devi. An old man, who boasted of having roughed 60 severe summers, said that his grandfather, who died at the age of 105 five years earlier, had seen Yogini Devi and that she was 80 or so then. Many others claimed to have had a glimpse of Yogini Devi from a distance. Proofs of Yogini Devi's presence on the hill came also from several simple shepherds who frequented the foot of the hill daily to graze their cattle. A few adventurous young men said they had seen a small temple of Lord Shiva there, well-kept, with regular worship. Many people talked about having received valuable help and guidance from Yogini Devi in mysterious ways. There was the case of a shepherd who, one afternoon, was asleep near the hills while his herds were grazing. He dreamt of a sheep having fallen into a well and its struggle for life. When he woke up startled, he did actually find one missing. He rushed to the well and with the assistance of a few persons from the nearby farm, rescued the poor animal.

No one in Adityana village had seen or talked to Yogini Devi. All the help and guidance attributed to her always came to the people of the village, and other occasional visitors, in the form of dreams. In all such dreams, people invariably saw a faint form of Yogini Devi. People's dreams were of different orders. There were dreams in which people recognized the events to come in the future and also those that gave others a clear peep into the past and the present.

To cite a few instances from the long list of succour people had received from Yogini Devi, the following authentic events can be included:

(1) The police Patel of the village was granted awareness in advance about a fatal fall from a tree top. It came correct.

(2) A local grocer clearly saw a dream in which his late grandparents were storing away valuables inside the made-to-order places of concealment in the house. Deft digging in the house got him what his ancestors had hidden.

(3) A native doctor from an adjacent village saw his kidnapped daughter being taken in Kirti Express, bound for Mehsana in Gujarat. The vision in the dream was so distinct that he even saw that his daughter was wet with nervous perspiration. He managed to overtake the train after chasing in a car and got the kidnappers nabbed and sent to jail.

Amongst numerous persons who got earthly benefits from Yogini Devi, there were quite a few who had the opportunity to receive spiritual treasure from Yogini Devi. But, unfortunately, as it generally happens in such cases, not all of them made use of these treasures.

The numerous accounts about Yogini Devi greatly amazed me. I became excited at the prospect of meeting such a powerful psychic personality. I felt that I should seek her permission before embarking upon the climb to meet her. So I began sending out concentrated thoughts of supplication so that she may grant my prayer, just as she had fulfilled the desires of others. I willed for a reply by midnight and actually believed that it would come.

Mystical Hills

I was all by myself on that Friday night, a few hours before midnight. My room in the village temple was small. And when the lights were turned out, the place became pitch dark. Light, as well all know, hinders one's pointed thinking, whereas darkness promotes calmness and concentration.

Around midnight, I began endeavouring to visualize Yogini Devi. I manoeuvred my mental sight to go over the hills. It didn't take me long to spot her serene figure, seated under a tree. I had a faint feeling of being invisibly aided and, suddenly, I caught sight of Makarana Sahib also emerging on the path leading to the tree under which Yogini Devi was seated. A little later, there were thought-flashes of assent for my climb up the hills, with a helpful hint to go up from the southern direction. Because I could not maintain mental composure any longer, I lost contact of the vision of the hill. Later, my repeated attempts to get reconnected failed.

Next morning, soon after the sunrise, I walked up to the foot of the hill, which was about two miles from the village, and began climbing from the southern side as directed. I had to do a good deal of criss-crossing on the hill to climb up.

Even with the several sloping ridges around, the place on the top of the hill was wide enough, flat, with thick closely knit clusters of trees and a heavy growth of vegetation. I moved directly to the tiny temple of Lord Shiva which was at the extreme eastern end of the hill and rested there for a while.

Nobody was near the temple. The temple appeared to have been recently washed and that the conventional rites of worship were performed there was also apparent.

The general atmosphere on top of the hill was peaceful and completely free from foul influences. The place filled me with the welcome warmth of inward peace. I got up and went inside the temple. Seating myself there, I did some breathing exercises and offered my prayers to the deity there.

After the prayers, I moved about all over the hill top without finding anyone. Thereafter, I did the obvious thing—waited for Yogini Devi.

The fleeting hours found me mentally restive and in that impatient frame of mind I began to wonder whether I would be able to see Yogini Devi at all or in the same form as I had seen her in the dream. In the dream I had seen her arrayed in a dazzling rich aura, her tall, thin, physical frame engulfed in an oval shaped spiral of bright yellow colour, with a disc shaped golden hue around her head. I have never had a dream more vivid than the one I have narrated.

Then, I heard the ruffling sound of someone or something coming across the ground, which was covered with dry leaves fallen from the trees. I turned back and saw a fair, feminine figure. Though aged, she was nimble footed and walked erect, with a staff in her hands, holding her head high. The weight of the years did not seem to lie too heavily upon her. Her slim body was covered by a thick garment made of barks of trees. The unkempt mass of hair which flowed from her square head was greyish and reached her knees. Her square head was a clear indication of her balanced brain with a fine ability for deductive reasoning. I was a trifle disappointed when I did not see her in alluring auric attire.

On the whole, however, I felt grateful and satisfied by her graceful bearing, radiating peace all over. As she came near, I prostrated at her holy feet. Then we went to a giant fig tree which was right behind the Shiva temple. She seated herself there on a shrub, and wiped the beads of sweat on her forehead. Speaking in Hindi, she said, "Sit, son."

The way Yogini Devi straightened herself and closed her eyes, it occurred to me that she was preparing for communion with distant souls. Quite a while later, she opened her sparkling eyes and slowly said, "Makarana Sahib had talked to me about your having met him in Mirpurkhas through Masthramji. Only last night, as you know, the good yogi was here. It was he who, through the powerful process of thought relays, first brought about requisite fluctuations in your brain pattern and then enabled you to vividly see us and also assisted you to receive the thought message from us."

"I know what all you desire to know about me and also the present whereabouts of Makarana Sahib and Masthramji. But then, however natural your inclination may be, I must make it clear to you, son, giving vent to curiosity and endeavouring to dig out the unproductive details about anyone isn't the way of a Sadhaka. A true aspirant should develop deep detachment and dispassionate disposition. Indulging in trivialities is a waste of time and energy."

As she left, I began to sense a slight shiver overtaking me and my limbs becoming heavy. From that state, I could very hazily see Yogini Devi gracefully walking away westwards, unmindful of what was happening to me. I became sleepy and dozed off, right there on the hill itself.

That night, when it was all quiet outside and when I was quiet within, as I lay on my usual bed, made of a bare sheet spread on the ground, I was suddenly seized with a light tremulous sensation all over my body. I knew it to be another attempt on the part of my astral body to get out. Within seconds, I perceived a mass of gaseous matter emanating from the umbilicus and going up, forming a shape similar to the size of my physical body. I felt in me the lightness of a piece of paper. Just at a point when I was reaching near the fifteen feet high ceiling of the room, I turned over involuntarily. It was then that I found myself connected to the gross body lying below.

The Chrystal Chime

Invisible souls are working for the welfare of humankind. Their spiritual radar is very powerful. Every call is flashed on their radar and they rush to help, at the behest of the High Command.

4

Your Dreams Are My Dreams

Our Dreams

>I look for a dream
>
>In the harvest moon,
>
>The song that was sung
>
>At the close of noon,
>
>In the fields of winter,
>
>In shacks of monsoon!
>
>I look for a dream
>
>In a flamingo star,
>
>The swing of birds
>
>The melody orb,
>
>In the cusp of future,
>
>In Zodiac signs
>
>Of magnetic murals,
>
>In the sky!
>
>I look for a dream
>
>In the Om of the Universe
>
>Tat sat . . . Sat tat,
>
>The vibration is the same!

Most of our life is spent in dreams. We dream in the night, when we are sleeping and we dream during the day, when we are awake. These two dreams are different. Some dreams, when we are sleeping, are puzzling; some dreams are persistent; some dreams are scary; and some dreams bring relief. In understanding of mystical events, every dream is subject to cause and effect. Every dream which is persistent, is Karmic.

We will discuss this more when we go through the extraordinary dreams of lay persons or extraordinary ways of mystics later in the book.

When Dreams Come True

Strange things happen through dreams, which appear as miracles. And miracles they are, indeed! Otherwise, how do you justify the travel of a painting by a great Japanese artist, travelling from Japan to Dubai?

Dr. Shirin is a practising gynaecologist, who is on the spiritual path. I met her at a friend's house. She was at that time living in Dubai, but was keen to serve India. Later she initiated the programme of service to humanity with her medical mission, "From Ganga Sagar to Gangotri". It was a programme of providing medical aid to the women living in the sub-Himalayan region.

On the spiritual side she is an ardent devotee of Shirdi Sai Baba. She calls herself "Sai Baba chamchi". She has done the reverential parikrama of the sacred mount Kailash, along with her husband Venkat. For several years she worked in England and Dubai. Currently, she lives in Pune, and besides being a reputed gynaecologist, she is also a yoga and meditation coach.

The Painting Flew from Mt. Fuji in Japan to Dubai

Seldom are miracles tangible. Recently, I came across a miracle regarding a tangible physical object, proof enough of the extraordinary energies that flow in this Universe. The physical object was a painting. It was hung between two other sacred paintings, in the main hall of Dr. Shirin's house. Of the three paintings, two were of Mt. Kailash. They looked familiar. But the third painting, in between the two, was a mystery. It bore the signature of the artist in Japanese characters. It was not only puzzling, but also interesting to find a Japanese painting in an Indian home, in between the Mt. Kailash paintings! When asked about the Japanese painting, Dr. Shirin smiled and said, I "It is a sacred painting." She then narrated the following mystical story:

> I was working in Dubai several years ago. On Christmas Eve, I received a call from a stranger. I was in the midst of dressing for a party. I was in a great rush and not keen to answer the phone call. The caller said, "I have a surprise gift for you. Where and when can I deliver it to you?"
>
> I had a busy and a tiring day. I was all set to relax that evening. To meet an unknown person was the last thing on my mind.
>
> "Can we meet this evening?" The caller asked politely. "I am in Dubai just for a day, and I have to see you before I leave," he explained.
>
> This put me in a dilemma. Should I invite him to my friend's party? On an impulse, I asked him, "Will you introduce yourself?"
>
> "I am Aiykama. I have come from Tokyo. It is my pleasure carrying this gift for you," he replied in a soft voice. He sounded as if it was an unusual honour for him to carry this gift for me.
>
> He explained that he was Japanese and arranged courses to be conduct in *Johre*. Johre is a technique of spiritual healing which uses the energy from the sun to heal. Based on a holistic approach towards the body, mind, and spirit, the energy from the sun is internalized to cure physical ailments.
>
> I was an ardent fan of Johre. As a doctor, I had attended several courses on the techniques of Johre. The workshops on the use of energy from the sun helped me to heal my patients faster.
>
> Suddenly, I realised that I had met Aiykama at one such workshop and I had been greatly impressed by his healing powers. By sheer coincidence, the party I was going to attend that evening was being hosted by a group of friends involved in Johre. I had no hesitation in inviting Aiyakama to the X'mas party. So I invited him and he said he would be delighted to attend a party being given by friends of Johre.

At the party, Aiykama told me about the painting he was carrying and which, as per his instructions, had to be gifted to me.

"Who had given this painting? Who has instructed you to carry it to me?" I asked, surprised. I did not know anyone in Japan who would send me a painting as a gift.

"The artist himself and his wife have given the painting."

"The artist?"

"It is a sacred painting."

"'It is very kind of you to have taken the trouble of carrying the gift for me. How can I accept a gift from a person I do not even know?" I asked, expressing my unwillingness to accept the painting.

During the party, I kept wondering who this strange artist was. Why did he and his wife send this gift to me? How best could I avoid accepting the gift?

"You have to accept this gift. It is a sacred painting, and you have the rare honour of receiving it," Aiyakama insisted.

I pulled Aiyakama aside, away from the tumult of music and chatter, and asked him to explain. Mr. Aiyakama, a typical Japanese Master, bowed to me graciously, sat down on a low stool and narrated the events which brought the gift to me.

"I had gone to Kyoto to attend a conference of Myshusan Okadwe Association. There I met an elderly couple – gentle, kind, and very pious. The husband is a famous painter and his wife is a practising psychologist. She has extraordinary psychic powers. It is this couple who has given me this precious gift for you," Aiyakama explained. I listened to him in rapt attention.

"They are an extremely well-known and popular couple in Japan. The gentleman is famous for his unique paintings and the lady for her stupendous psychic powers. This artist paints only one picture of Mount Fuji in a year. There are people in

Japan who save money throughout the year to be able to buy this sacred painting. This year, too, he painted the picture of Mount Fuji. Just a day before the auction of this great work, his wife had a dream. In the dream she saw an Indian couple, with two sons. They lived in a place which looked like Dubai. She saw the young couple healing many patients, with loving kindness. She was touched by their spiritual sadhna. This year's painting, she was asked by the Divine mysterious voice from the Beyond, should be gifted to the doctor couple. So the auction was called off this year. At the conference the artist's wife asked me if I knew of any such a couple in Dubai. She described the couple in detail. I told her that I knew such a couple, Dr. Shirin and her husband. Then she requested, 'Please, next time you visit Dubai, do take this painting to them. But don't forget to bring the photographs of the couple. I want to confirm whether it is the same couple who the Higher voice has ordained me to give this painting as a gift.'"

I was hesitant; the gift was very expensive and worth a small fortune.

Seeing my discomfort, Aiyakama tried to convince me, saying, "It is for good luck. It is an extremely precious gift. It is a divine gift."

I finally decided to accept the gift as a sign of good luck.

"I must take pictures to be taken back to Japan. The artist and his wife have requested. They want to make sure the gift goes to the right person," said Aiyakama. So we had photographs taken, with the painting.

When I took the painting home, I found something amazing.

This was the painting of Mt. Fuji. I already had two paintings of Mt. Kailash. One had Om written in calligraphy in snow, and the other showed the pencil like peak of the sacred Kailash. Amazingly, between the two paintings was a space with a nail, as if the space was reserved for the sacred painting gifted to me. And the gifted painting fitted beautifully in there. I put the painting there. With the sacred painting in the middle of the two paintings of Mt. Kailash, the wall looked complete.

"Mysterious are the ways of God. How this divine gift found its way from Japan to Dubai, to the right place on the wall, is still a mystery to me," said Dr. Shirin.

And yes, the photograph of the Dr. Shirin, taken when she received the sacred painting, matched with the image seen by the painter's wife in the vision. Aiyakama confirmed this on reaching Japan a few days later.

The Crystal Sounds

Be not afraid of dreams! Dreams can show you the path which God has ordained for you. Dreams can guide you to do certain acts which are the wish of the Supreme. There are different types of dreams. If we understand them, we will not be afraid of them, but welcome them as tools of achieving our desires.

Kamala's Story: Chhota Hemkunt

Built through a dream—and what a coincidence!
Hemkunt is the holy place of the Sikhs. Located in the Himalayas, Hemkunt is the sacred site above the Valley of Flowers, where Guru Govind Singh had meditated in his previous birth. Various Sikh scriptures describe him as descending to earth riding a white horse. It is said he was a Yogi who received the command to descend to the plains to protect Hindus against the torture of invaders. A miniature replica of Hemkunt is built near Pune. But the way this Gurudwara was built is amazing. It was through a dream! And not one dream, but two dreams!

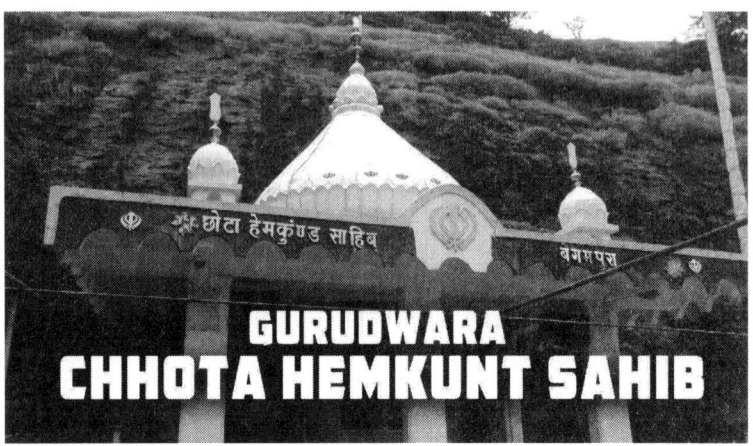

Gurudwara Chhota Hemkunt Sahib Begampura (Maharashtra)

The phone rang for the third time.

Instinctively, I knew the call was from my sister Kamala, living in Mumbai. For the last three months Kamala had been calling me regularly in the morning. She was obsessed with a dream, and a bit scared, why she saw it every night, at the same time. In the dream she saw a Gurudwara being made in the hills around Pune, and that she was present there, wearing white clothes. It was all a dream, but she could physically experience it. She described every minute detail every time she phoned me, and requested me to search for this Gurudwara.

At first I advised her to forget about it. A dream is a dream. The entire world is a dream. But she insisted — she had to find a reason for the dream.

"Did you find out?" She asked me every time she called.

"Not yet," I would confess.

"Go and look for it around the hills of Pune."

My enquiries with the people I knew who were living in the suburbs of Pune yielded no clue.

"When will you find out?" was her urgent query.

"No one here seems to know about it."

"Take a car, drive to the north or wherever required and check out. You have to locate this Gurudwara," she pleaded with me. Why, I could not understand. Yet an order from an elder sister is an order. You simply cannot ignore it. But I did not wish to take the trouble of driving into the hills, merely on the basis of dreams, to search for a Gurudwara which was being built or already built by then.

Then, one evening my husband's niece, who lived in Nigdi, visited us.

"You know," she said, full of excitement, "Yesterday we went to a Gurudwara. It was very beautiful. It is in the hills beyond Dehu road."

"You visited a Gurudwara in the hills?" I asked, surprised.

"Yes, it is in a cave," she replied. "I and my friends went for the inauguration. It is situated beyond Pawana Dam."

I immediately called up Kamala and told her that a Gurudwara in a cave was inaugurated recently. Could it be the same one she had the dream about?

"I myself wish to see and verify it, but my health does not permit me to travel. I am sure it is the same Gurudwara which I continue to see regularly in my dreams," she said. She earnestly requested me to visit the place, as the dream of the Gurudwara was persistent, clear, and vivid to the extent of identifying the colour of every stone and every picture there.

"The Gurudwara is in a cave of black stone and it has a forest around it which is quite dense," she said.

I was wondering how to go to the remote location where the Gurudwara was, when one weekend my husband said, "I will come with you. Let us start now itself."

And so Arjan and I got into the car. On the way we saw a Gurudwara at Khadki village. "The best way to reach there is to take the directions from the Gurudwara at Nigdi," said the pious Panthi of Khadki. We did not go to the Nigdi, but headed directly for Pawana village, after crossing the Pawana Dam. Luckily for us, the village had grown and become larger in the last year and a half, and the villagers had heard about the Gurudwara.

While buying a packet of biscuits at a shop in the village, my husband asked for directions. The shopkeeper pointed out the way to us. But when we reached the place where we had to take a turn, there was no sign about which way to go for the Gurudwara. Just then a bus stopped and a villager got down. He showed us an unpaved road through the forest, which he said would take us there.

As we drove down the road, there was no sign of habitation anywhere. After two kilometres, we almost came to a dead end at a small hut. The hut was locked. There was a padlock on its door. We took a chance and went behind the hut. A young village woman was washing clothes. "Just go behind this hillock. The Gurudwara is there," she said.

We could not believe it, because the path was narrow and covered with bushes. It opened on a rectangular piece of land which has no signboard. But we went, anyway.

Just behind the hillock was the most amazing site. On the slope of the hill was a village. Down below, there was a small dam on the stream, which had formed a lake. On the top was a Sikh flag fluttering in the air.

We walked by a terraced garden. Half a dozen tractors were parked near a cattle shed. A small farmhouse stood below the Gurudwara.

To our surprise, the Gurudwara was inside a black cave, its interiors exactly as described by Kamala. It was a mystical moment for me.

As we were leaving, an elderly Sikh couple came out of the farmhouse and invited us in. It was the day of the Maharashtrian New Year and the couple was expecting villagers to come for lunch. We declined the invitation for lunch, but said tea was welcome.

As we were having our tea, we got into a conversation with the couple. The gentleman was a Rotarian and, as a part of the club project, they had adopted a nearby hamlet, where people were below the poverty line.

While we discussed the place, its location, and our difficulty in finding it, the lady asked me, "Who informed you about Gurudwara?"

"My sister," I replied.

"She lives in Pune?"

"No. She leaves in Mumbai, Andheri."

"How did she know?"

"She had a dream. For the last two years she has been phoning me regularly to find out the Gurudwara in a black cave."

"Dream?" she asked surprised, "Your sister had a dream of this Gurudwara two years ago?"

"Maybe two and half years ago," I said. "And the dream kept repeating every few days."

"That's when I, too, had the dream. I had a dream asking me to build a Gurudwara. It was a mystical dream." The lady opened up and started talking frankly.

Build a new Gurudwara? Where? How? These questions bothered her. But she hesitated to disclose her dream to her family members, fearing they would ridicule her. Around the same time, Mouni Baba of Nanded was visiting Nigdi Gurudwara, near her home. She confided in Mouni Baba about the dream. She told him she had the same dream three times, on consecutive nights, around the same time every night.

Mouni Baba did not say anything at that time. The next morning he visited their home around 9 a.m.

"I was in the midst of morning cooking. Mouni Baba said he wished to go to our farmhouse. I left my cooking, and my husband and I went along with Mouni Baba immediately.

Once we reached there, Babaji took a stroll in front of the shed at the foot of hill. He gazed at the far off mountains, took another stroll, and then pointing to a huge black rock, indicated the site of the new Gurudwara to be built. My husband and I decided to follow his instructions and build the Gurudwara at that place."

"We had difficulty in blasting the rock. It took us a long time. We had to hire an agency to do it. What you saw as the cave was one big black rock. It had to be pulled out as a whole."

"Yes, and it fell out as one single piece creating the cave for the 'manji' to be enshrined," I completed the description of the blast.

"How did you know?"

"Not me, but my sister Kamala. She said she was witnessing the whole event. She was the figure in white — and when the black rock fell, someone, her Guardian Angel, pushed her aside and saved her."

The lady smiled. "That was me. I was standing outside, here. When the rock fell, it was me . . . the lady was wearing a white salwar kameez."

I took a few pictures of the cave and the Gurudwara and sent them to Kamala.

Kamala recognised the temple from the pictures. "It is the same temple I see in my dreams. Thank you so much. Now I can sleep in peace," she said.

Her dreams stopped troubling her after she sent some money for charity to the Gurudwara.

This was around five years ago. To this day, Kamala insists that she was present at the time of the blasting of the black rock. "In the bygone days, a messenger of Guru Nanak Dev must have halted there and prayed. I am sure about that!" she says.

Other Temples Built through Dreams

Are there dream incidents similar to Chhota Hemkunt? There is one here in Kolkata — the Adyapith Ma Kali temple. "This temple is unique, both in terms of architecture and symbolism", writes Seema Burman in Sunday *Speaking Tree*. "Made of white marble, it is actually three temples in one." It is here that she felt the presence of Sri Ramakrishna Paramhans.

The temple is a devotee's dream come true. In the dream, Sri Ramakrishna said to his devotee, Ananda, to shave, bathe in the river, and then go to Eden Garden and find the Divine Mother at a particular spot. Ananda found the idol of Ma Kali at the spot indicated in the dream.

"I am Adyashakti (primordial force) and I am to be worshipped as Adya Ma," was the message of Ma Kali in the dream. Ananda recorded his dream in his book, *Swapna-Jevan*, before he left this earth in 1929.

The Dakshineshwar Temple was built by a successful Ayurveda doctor, Ananda Bhattacharya, as a result of a series of dreams of Ma Kali and Sri Ramakrishna Paramhans, in the year 1915.

5

Mystical Dreams

*Live the full life of the mind, exhilarated by
new ideas, intoxicated by
the romance of the unusual.*

Ernest Hemmingway

To Dream or Not to Dream

The human mind is beautiful. It has several layers. Two important ones are the conscious mind and the sub-conscious mind. The conscious mind has the ability to sleep, the sub-conscious mind remains awake all the time. When the conscious mind is sleeping, the sub-conscious mind keeps working, naturally, automatically. The conscious mind is a "thought" machine. It thinks, creates, and analyses thoughts. In a positive state, the sub-conscious helps to find solutions to problems via dreams. The sub-conscious mind, in its "higher" wakeful state, also witnesses the phenomenon of happenings in the Universe. It is already connected with it because it has symbolic relationship with the universal mind.

Time is a thought concept. The past, the present, and the future is one stream. Time is timeless. It is the flow of eternity. Some of the dreams convey the events yet to come, or yet to happen. They pertain to the phenomenon which takes the physical form at a later date, and which is to be witnessed or experienced by the conscious mind at a distant space.

Types of Dreams

Psychologists, clairvoyants, and holy persons divide dreams into five categories.
1) Dead dreams, 2) Predictive or Premonition dreams, 3) Advisory dreams, 4) Communicative dreams, and 5) Novel dreams.

Dead dreams: This type of dream pertains to events that have already taken place in the past or in the distant past. These dreams are sometimes clear and show your previous birth locations, buildings, and people. Sometimes these dreams are jumbled, unrelated, and fleeting. The dead dreams are meaningless, unless they are repeated and persistent. Some of these dreams keep repeating and you wake up, remembering

Mystical Dreams

the dream clearly. They may indicate Karmic links of your previous births. But, as we all know, past is dust! Such dreams are "dead" and of no consequence. We all experience dead dreams many times.

Predictive or Premonition dreams: These dreams often come as a warning of an impending worldly incident. Simple desert people and simple hill people often get dreams of prediction. Red Indians in the West Coast, USA, could experience a storm 24 hours before it happened.

These dreams pertain to the future. They are warning signals and help you to avert a disaster or an unwanted incident. They pertain to things yet to happen. People who live by the wisdom of heart often get such dreams.

Advisory dreams: There is not much of a difference between advisory dreams and predictive dreams. Advisory dreams help to solve the problems which the conscious mind is not able to sort out. Advisory dreams are in the nature of guidance. Sometimes the Guru helps the disciple through such dreams. Strictly rational people do not have dreams of this sort.

Communicative dreams: These dreams are very strange. They are interlinked with many other humans, visible and invisible. These are dreams where souls from the other world communicate with the living. These communications are for spiritual progress of those on earth. Compassion of the invisible souls drives them to communicate with those on earth who flounder in the absence of light.

Novel dreams: These are truly "mystical" dreams. In these dreams, the dreamer actually witnesses what is happening elsewhere. My sister Kamala's dream of the Gurudwara falls in this category. She insists she was there, in a white dress, witnessing the blast and the formation of the cave, which enshrined the Adi Granth. These kinds of dreams come to highly pious persons or those who do regular meditation and are on the spiritual path. They are the dreams of those dreaming of higher things in life.

Dream Box on My Shelf

In my dream box of mails, three dreams are posted. Asha's dream, Rukmani's dream, and Ujwala's dream.

Asha's Dream

Let's dream more and more . . .

Asha is a retired professor of Marathi. Very recently, she narrated the following experience at a meeting of the college girls where she used to work.

> I would like to share my dream of Sadhu Vaswani. I had been teaching here for a while. At that time I was passing through a very difficult phase of my life. My marriage was in doldrums. I was also facing other problems like finance, health, and family dislocation, etc. I used to be very disturbed and upset. At such times, I used to go to Sadhu Vaswani's kutiya. I had seen him being lifted in a chair by four devotees when he was alive. I did not have much communication with him, though he did bless me whenever I met him.
>
> One night I had a dream. Sadhu Vaswani came in my dream and, as usual, he put his hand on my head and shook it. When he removed his hand, I was still feeling something on my head. When I put my hand on my head I felt something there. There was Om in my hand.
>
> I do not know the meaning of that dream, but since that day I have strong faith in Sadhu Vaswani.

So, dear readers, dream on. Be not afraid of dreams, for dreams are the stuff of which life is made!

Rukmani's Dream

Let me describe Rukmani's dream.

> Rukmani was a strong, brave woman. She faced the problems during the partition of the country in 1947 with a rare grit and fortitude. Later, she even sold off her bangles during a severe financial crisis in the family. But a time came when she was surrounded by tragedies. During that period of one year, when there were two deaths and a broken engagement in the

family, she was fully shattered. Being a pious woman, she did not lose her faith, but she was in great distress. While she was at the bottom of the dark abyss, she had a dream.

The dream was as clear as the day. A saintly person, lean and frail, with a flowing white beard, appeared in a vision, giving her prasad. He said, "Take this prasad and be blessed." Since she had not seen him before, she asked, in the dream itself, "Who are you?" He replied, "I am Baba Govind Das." The dream then ended. But Rukmani's curiosity did not end with the dream. She checked with relatives, friends, and spiritual seekers whether they knew any Baba Govind Das. But she drew a blank.

Three months passed by. The family members dismissed the dream as a figment of her imagination. Then one evening, a cousin visited her. As is the custom among many families to offer food and drink to a visitor, Rukmani said to him, "Please have dinner before you leave." The cousin showed great hurry to go. "No, I cannot wait," he said, "I have another commitment." Rukmani did not give up. She tried to use her persuasion powers, but in vain. "Oh dear, I cannot. I have to rush to Dadar railway station to receive my Guru," he said.

"Your Guru? What is his name?" Rukmani asked immediately.

"He is known by the name of Baba Govind Das."

Rukamni's joy knew no bounds. "I am coming with you right now," she said excitedly.

"The Dadar railway station platform is very crowded, my dear sister. You will not be able to step there. Besides, how will you return home so late all alone? It is not safe," the cousin tried to dissuade her. Seeing her sad face, he said, "O.K., I shall come tomorrow morning and take you to my Guru. But just tell me, why do you want to meet him?"

"Because three months ago, he came into my dream to comfort me."

Everyone sitting around was stunned.

Next morning, as promised, Rukmani's cousin came to pick her up. Together, they went to Sion (in Mumbai) to Halani Darbar*. Rukmani waited impatiently outside the room where Baba was sitting. The moment she entered, Baba's eyes held her. He was the same saint she had seen in her dream. Baba gave her prasad and asked her name as if he was meeting her for the first time.

Rukmani stood before him, speechless. She nodded slowly as if to say "Thank you!"

Ujwala's Dream

Ujwala is a simple, rustic girl. She lives with us, taking care of the house and the kitchen. She is as temperamental as the phases of the moon. Every morning she wakes up and talks of her "dream", requesting for an interpretation.

Some time ago she had a dream, which we disbelieved then.

I returned home from work one day, tired and exhausted.

"Please ring up Chachi in K.L. (Kuala Lumpur, Malaysia)," she ordered me, even before I could put down my books and my bag.

"I will, I will," I assured her.

An hour passed.

"Did you call up Chachi?" she asked sternly. "Please call her."

"Why?" I asked, trying to avoid the call. She literally pleaded that I call Chachi.

"But why? Did they call up?" I asked her angrily. I was fed up with her pestering me to make a long distance call to my brother-in-law's family.

"I had a dream this morning," Ujwala said.

---

* A Darbar (assembly) is a typical ashram with a living guru presiding over it. It adopts the name of its geographical location. Halani Darbar gets its name from the Sindh town of Halan, where more than a hundred years ago this Darbar was established.

"What's new about it?"

"I saw Chachi fall and taken to hospital."

"So? What time?"

"It was early, I think it was 5.30 or 6 a.m.," she said.

"It was 8.30 a.m. or 9 a.m. in K.L. at that time. Do you think that you were seeing the whole incident while it was happening thousands of miles away in K.L.?" I asked. Ujwala's face fell. Just to please her, I called up K.L. Chachi's daughter, Priya, picked up the phone. After exchanging pleasantries, I asked very casually, "How is Chachi?" In the meantime, my brother-in-law took the phone and said, "Chachi is fine."

"Where is she? Can I speak to her?"

"She is in the other room resting. I will ask her to call you back in the morning," he said and he kept the phone down. It was 8 p.m. in K.L. at that time. Chachi normally went to bed at midnight. I was slightly angry with Ujwala for pestering me the whole afternoon after I returned from the college at 2 p.m., and not allowing me to lie down and rest, while Chachi was peacefully resting in K.L.

A few months later, my brother-in-law's family visited us. While chatting with Chachi, I told her about Ujwala's dream and how she pestered me to call her, but she was resting peacefully in her room.

"It was eight o'clock in K. L. when you called. I was sleeping in the room next to the hall because I had just returned from the hospital. I had felt dizzy in the morning around 8.30 a.m. and I had fallen down unconscious. Everyone was worried and I was rushed to the hospital."

"And in the hospital you were put on saline?"

"Yes. How do you know?" Chachi asked intrigued.

"Ujwala's dream. Didn't I tell you, she pestered me to call you that day? This is exactly the sequence Ujwala described while telling us about her dream."

Ujwala had, on earlier occasions, too, dreamt about Chacha and Chachi's family. For example, they were shifting to new premises or a new place of work, and she had described in detail the location of the place where they were shifting.

We all are connected. We all have a symbiotic relationship. We are all a part of that Consciousness which is universal. In simple words, there is One in All, and All in One.

The Crystal Chime

Get tuned to nature. But first purify your mind. Be natural. Live by the heart, not by reason. That shall make you receptive to the guidance coming from the invisible sources in dreams.

Saints, too, at first receive the blueprint from the Above, and they act accordingly They appear in dreams, they say things to you through others, and they may even communicate with you through their high frequency vibrations. Saints seldom use words. They pass on the messages to other sadhaks who go out to fulfil their tasks.

It is said of the poet Rumi that his poetry was the communication through the stream of Divine Light which flows through the Universe.

Crystal Meditation Chime (Silver)

6

Secrets of Miracles

The Jasmine Flower

Vijaya is a beautician turned *pranic* healer. She is also a versatile singer and writer. This transformation came through intense personal suffering. She became a Sai *bhakt*. She has a Guru in Kolkata.

I first met Vijaya when she was a beautician. She wanted coverage in a woman's magazine, which I represented in Pune at that time. Later, when she got into Om therapy, she volunteered to teach it at some of the educational institutes I was connected with.

She has this miracle story to share with us.

> I was eighteen years old then. I was a trained beautician and I worked with Figurette Beauty Parlour on Janglee Maharaj Road, Pune.
>
> One morning, I opened the parlour as usual and was waiting for clients. I decided to get some fresh air before the day began. I went to the door and stood there. Suddenly, I saw an unusually tall sadhu with a huge turban on the pavement across the road. He had fierce eyes and looked scary. Instinctively, I turned my face away. Anyway, he was on the other side of the road and partially covered by the bus stand shelter. He saw me and kept staring at me.
>
> I did not want to go inside the parlour. I did not want him to get the feeling that I was afraid of him. There was something in him which mesmerised me and I could not move. Then, this tall sadhu walked across the road and came over to me. He sensed that I was scared. Without smiling, he said, "So you are a Sai Bhakt?" The moment he uttered the word "Sai", I felt relieved. I think he noticed my ease, for he said, "Will you not invite me in?" I stood there perplexed and totally lost as to what to reply. "Can I come in? Bring one piece of paper," he said. I searched for a blank sheet of paper. A beauty parlour has creams, lotions, aroma oils. But a piece of white paper? Surprisingly, I found a blank sheet of white paper. "Tear it into half," he said. I did so. "Now take one piece of the paper and fold it. Hold it tight in your fist. Close your eyes."

At this point I said, "I will not close my eyes." True, I did not look even once into his eyes. I avoided direct eye contact with him for the fear of being hypnotized. I kept my eyes open, vacantly looking here and there. He recited some mantras. He was murmuring all the while I held the piece of paper in my hand.

After some time, I started getting the fragrance of jasmine flowers. I love the fragrance of jasmine flowers. I wondered where the fragrance was coming from. After ten minutes or so of that "stillness" he said, "Open your hand." The moment I opened my hand, the room was filled with jasmine fragrance. "Now unfold the paper" he said. I unfolded the paper held tightly in my fist. Surprise of surprise, it had a beautiful white jasmine flower. A real jasmine flower. "Take it home," he said. "You are a Sai bhakt. I am also a Sai bhakt. When I come to your house do not turn me away."

And he was gone.

I took the flower home and gave it to my mother. She kept it in her pooja room. The jasmine flower was there till recently — till my mother passed away.

"Did the sadhu visit you again?" I asked her.
"No, never." Vijaya replied.
"Then?"
"In our family, we do not turn away anyone who visits us. We offer food to every visitor knocking on the door. This is what the sadhu wanted to say. This is what he meant. Perhaps that is the true meaning of being a Sai Bhakt."

The Crystal Window Opens

The occult art of materializing things out of nothing has been practised in India since ancient times. In this context, many stories have been written in India and abroad. The following wisdom nugget is worth reading.

Rumi was a great Sufi poet. Once Rumi transformed an ordinary stone into what appeared to be a ruby. The "stone" turned into ruby was taken to a jeweller by one of the disciples and sold for thousands of rupees. When devotees complained to Rumi of what had happened, Rumi said, "It is wonderful for a layman to see copper being converted into a ruby and use it so. But more striking is the fact that the layman who uses it for material gains, himself is being transmitted from ruby into copper through his lack of true knowledge."

Duplicate, Triplicate, and Selfie

A rare historical incident: Shivaji Maharaj

If you ever visit Jamnagar, the erstwhile princely state of Jadejas, you will hear of many strange and fascinating stories of ghosts, apparitions, of a white woman walking from one Darghah to another. These stories are recorded and testified by teachers, and even rational scientists.

Jamnagar is the only town where the crematorium is a picnic spot, a place where you make merry while the dead bodies are cremated. If you are lucky, you may also hear of a saint who "ether doubled" to help his devotees in road accidents. If these stories are the common repertoire in Saurashtra, the historical, proven incidents of mysterious types are common in Maharashtra. Although Shivaji Maharaj, the Maratha warrior king, has a place in history books, very few know of the mystical happenings in his life.

> Once, after fighting a fierce battle, Shivaji Maharaj was returning home. On the way he rested by the river side. He saw leaves with something written on them floating down stream. He picked them and found messages and mantras of wisdom written on them. Out of curiosity he followed the leaves and arrived at Sajjan ghat. There, on the river bank, in a small shelter sat a Mahatma. Out of reverence, he went to him and sought his blessings. As is the case with saints, the Mahatma, Samartha Ramdas, asked him to have food.

The Secrets of Miracles

"I am not alone; I have an army of soldiers, horses, and elephants resting on the river bank."

"I have food for all of them, call them," replied the Mahatma. Shivaji looked around and wondered from where the food would come for his large army.

Soon, the Mahatma called a devotee and asked him to remove the stone covering the mouth of the cave. When the devotee removed the stone, Shivaji was stunned. The cave was full of delicious food for him and the soldiers. There was food for the animals, by the side. Shivaji Maharaj had the delicious food, fit for a king. The army and the animals also had a hearty fill.

Shivaji expressed surprise at the variety of food prepared in a short time.

"How did you do it?" he asked.

"Go and meet a Mahatma called Tukaram. He lives in Dehu Road."

Shivaji, busy with his conquests, forgot all about the Mahatma Tukaram. Once, while travelling towards north, he came across the sign "Dehu Road" and remembered what Sant Ramdas had told him. He went along with his army to the tiny hut of Sant Tukaram, who later became his Guru. The rest is history.

Here is another story about Shivaji.

Once, Shivaji Maharaj was chased by the Mughal soldiers who were asked to kill Shivaji and take his dead body to the Emperor at Delhi. Shivaji Maharaj tried to escape, and then sought refuge with Sant Tukaram.

At that time, Sant Tukaram was preparing to sit for Kirtan. He told his congregation not to move till the Kirtan was over. Shivaji also sat among the congregation, hiding himself among the poor farmers. The Mughal soldiers following close on his heels, reached Dehu Road. Sant Tukaram sat still with eyes closed. Shivaji wanted to escape, but his Guru Sant Tukaram had asked the villagers not to move while the Kirtan was on. The Kirtan continued.

Shivaji thought, this was his end. Just then, a little distance away, a horse with the rider in Shivaji's garb galloped past and disappeared into the forest in the opposite direction. The Mughal army, seeing Shivaji on the galloping horse, turned back and went after the horse and its rider in the opposite direction. The Kirtan continued for a long time. When Shivaji was out of danger, Sant Tukaram opened his eyes and told the villagers to disperse.

Shivaji Maharaj fell at the feet of his Guru. Till this day, no one has been able to explain this incident. But it happened and happened for sure.

Saints have this Siddhi of duplicating even triplicating, but they do not use it unless ordained by the High Command!

Baba Nebhraj: The Mystery of Ether Double

My mother had met Baba Nebhraj a couple of times in 1946-47. Probably she had met him in Nawabshah, Sindh. She and another member of the family often regaled the family with his crazy ways of blessing the devotees. He did so by rhyming the name with wisdom words, such as, "Asha, you are truly a Bhasha; do not make Tamasha."

But the story my mother told my brother and I, when we were very young, was of his "ether double" which, incidentally, is recorded by many writers and historians of his time.

Nebhraj was a humble teacher in a primary school. He enjoyed the legacy of Sufi saints Bedyil and Bekas; of Paru Shah and Vasan Shah.

This incident refers to 1911. His school had its annual inspection. Nebhraj spent the early morning hours in meditation and prayer.

On the morning of the inspection, he was so engrossed in meditation and immersed in the Divine stream that he lost track of time. By the time he reached the school, it was too late. The inspection was over and the inspector had already left the school.

As soon as Nebhraj reached the school, the teachers told him that the Head Master had called for him. Nebhraj became nervous. He feared for the worst. When he reached the Head Master's office, the Head Master rose and congratulated him. "The inspector was very happy with your class. The students answered all his questions. Moreover, he was impressed by the discipline and the way you handled students."

In the Teachers Room everyone complimented him on his performance. He was the best teacher.

Nebhraj was surprised. How could this happen? He was not there in the school, yet everyone told him that he was there and had done a good job.

Nebhraj returned home and wrote his resignation letter. He kept aside his school clothes — pant, shirt, turban and a tie. Wearing a simple pyjama kurta, he renounced the world to serve the Ultimate Master, who had saved his honour and reputation.

The Crystal Chime

Saints do not perform Siddhis. They work through prayer or contact with the Master of all miracles!

7

Miracle Tools

Siddhis

Siddhis *are ancient skills.* Siddhis are paranormal powers. These powers and energies are acquired through the practise of yoga in various forms. The ancient scriptures like Upanishads describe the various Siddhis and the way they can be acquired. According to some sages, there are more than 120 Siddhis and these can be acquired through yogic exercises.

The siddhi energies work only on the physical plane. According to Hindu philosophy, which has a scientific base, the physical world is governed by physical energies. Hence these energies can govern and command physical objects. The physical objects may be ashes materialized from the air, or a flower created inside a paper, or other physical objects produced at will.

The word "siddhi" is derived from the Sanskrit word "sidh", which means perfection or attainment. It is mentioned in Upanishads, Mahabharat, and Buddhist canons. According to Hindu philosophy, there are eight Primary Siddhis:

1. Anima: Reducing one's body to the size of an atom
2. Mahima: Expanding one's body to a large size
3. Garima: Becoming heavy
4. Laghiana: Becoming almost weightless
5. Prapti: Having access to all places
6. Prakamya: Realizing whatever one desires
7. Istva: Possessing absolute Lordship
8. Vastava: The power to subjugate

Siddhis of Black Magic

The knowledge of Siddhis is very ancient, going back a thousand years. Maybe, over time, these energies, which were the result of spiritual sadhna, lost their true character and as they were manipulated into black magic, they became largely associated with Nath Panth yogis, as mentioned in Guru Nanak's stories of Balu and Mardana.

> Guru Nanak was meditating in the Himalayan mountains. It is said that one day Mardana felt very hungry. He went in search of food in the valley. There, the yogis made fun of his black ballooning dress. The yogis and yoginis "changed" Mardana into a black buffalo. Guru Nanak, by his spiritual powers, turned him back into human form.
>
> The Nath yogis were surprised. They wanted to know the secret science of reversing the effect of black magic. Guru Nanak spoke to them of the Supreme Being who had all the power in the Universe. The yogis pleaded with him to describe such a great miracle man. It is then Guru Nanak recited for them "Eko Onkar Kartar Purukh Nirbhae Nirve, Akal Murat Ajuni Sain Ba."

Swami Vivekanand's First Fascination

We have heard of Vivekananda, who witnessed many Siddhis. Here is one story:

> Once Swami Vivekananda, then known by his earlier name Narendra, was travelling in South India. There he heard of a yogi who could materialize objects out of nothing. Narendra was a rationalist. He did not believe that any person could materialize objects or things from thin air. He went to meet the yogi and challenged him to do the miracle in his presence. The yogi agreed. Narendra took him to an empty room, where he made him remove his clothes, and gave him his blanket to cover himself. Thus Narendra ensured that the room was empty and that the yogi had nothing on his person. He then closed the room. A few of Narendra's admirers were also present.

The yogi asked them to write on a slip of paper whatever they wished to eat, fold the paper, and keep it with them. It was a cold winter day. To test the powers of the yogi, some wrote "mango", others wrote "watermelon", "muskmelon", and so on. Even Narendra wrote one of the fruits unavailable in winter.

After they had finished writing, they kept their papers with them, without showing to anyone. Soon enough, the yogi produced mangoes, watermelons, bananas, muskmelons, and so on, from under the blanket. He produced them in large numbers.

Swami Vivekananda was wonderstruck. When he returned to Kolkata, he went to meet his Master, Swami Ramakrishna Paramhansa, a highly realized soul, who asked Swami Vivekanand, "Do you want to learn Siddhis? How many Siddhis do you want to learn?"

Swami Vivekananda replied, "No, Siddhis are not for me."

The Siddhi Performer: A Web of Secrets

Siddhis, as mentioned earlier, are techniques acquired during sadhna. Siddhis are extraordinary powers. The yogis, through concentration, combined with pranayama techniques, control the physical body, including thirst, hunger, excretion, etc.

The story of Prahalad Jani, which appeared in the *Outlook* magazine on 24 May, 2010, took scientists by surprise. Power-yoga performer Prahalad Jani, claimed his devotees, had not eaten or drunk water for the last 70 years. He had not excreted nor urinated in this period. The common people assumed he was a miracle man. But those with the wisdom of higher knowledge understood that he was practising various yoga techniques (Sadhna yoga), which made it possible for his conscious mind to control his physical body. The scientists of the New Delhi based Defence Institute of Physiology wanted to investigate the scientific truth so as to use it for practical purposes in the ice capped mountains, where jawans and soldiers have to live for months, often without regular supply of water and food.

For this purpose Jani, popularly called Mataji, who was 82 years old in 2010, was requested to undergo a medical examination. Jani was admitted for ten days in November 2013. He was also examined by a team of doctors at Sterling Hospital, Ahmedabad. Jani underwent many tests. No food, no water was given to him. The doctors and the neuro scientists were dumbstruck when they requested him to produce a urine sample of 50 ml. He produced 100 ml of urine in his bladder. He gave 50 ml to the pathologists for examination and absorbed the rest in his body.

When questioned on how this happened, Jani replied, "It is all Shakti. You cannot make it. You have to tap it."

The question is, how do you develop and build such Shakti? Can one do so through sadhna? Or through yoga techniques? Through sadhna and yoga techniques, one can obtain full knowledge of the physical body. This can be done by concentrating on the navel.

In Vibhuti Pada of Patanjali yoga, it is written that by performing *samayama* on the gullet, the cessation of hunger and thirst happens. The sensations of hunger and thirst depend on the secretions of glands. Knowledge of the working of these glands and the capacity to regulate their secretion gives power to the yogi to control the sensation. The prana controls the secretion of glands. By controlling and regulating the prana, a yogi is able to control his hunger and thirst.

The Crystal Bell

To enhance the physical feats of your body, and to cope up with the needs of today's environment of stress and strain, try regulating your breath.

Breathing control is the great secret mastered by Indian yogis. Every breath is divine and reverberates in the Universe. Physical feats can be performed, and wish-fulfilment attained, through regulating the breath.

Getting Out of the Trap

Sadhna

We live in a cocoon of "Little self" floating on a wave of negative emotions. The Universe is unending. To free oneself from this cocoon, and to be a happy flying butterfly, we need to practise Sadhna.

Today, with the growing restlessness of mind and an inner sense of insecurity, the need for meditation is great. Meditation has become the general medicine for humankind. Human beings need a respite from the world of hectic activities and perpetual restlessness of the mind. Mind, which is a composition of thoughts, is like a stream of water running in different directions. Call it a galloping horse or a drunken monkey; it plays the same tantrums and truants, irrespective of your individual identity as a person. But the same mind, when trained to run a race, will bring accolades and rewards. To train the mind is as difficult as to rein in a wild or runaway horse. Patience and practise can control it with spiritual and psychological techniques.

One of these techniques is meditation. Meditation can earn you that most sought after illusive thing called, "peace of mind". To draw a simile, mind is like a wayward stream or river of water, running to lower regions wherever it can. But if you build a dam on the higher regions, you can generate powerful electricity from the stream

There are several well tried types of meditation, ranging from Goenka's Vipassna technique to a simple ten minute Nirmala Devi's "touch, thank, and forgive" meditation. You have to choose what suits your body, mind, and soul. Remember, in matters of the spirit, intent is very powerful.

Today's life guidance gurus offer 3 formulae for a happy and healthy living. The three ingredients in their kit of "Meditation" techniques are: 1) Prana, 2) Yogic Kriya, and 3) Affirmation. Add to this the psycho-exercise of creative visualization. This mix works well for beginners.

You may ask, What is the relation between Sadhna and miracles?

The inner life influences the outer life.

Sadhna purifies and provides clarity of mind, better perception and focus. It also hones your intuition and clears the way for your latent desires to turn into actual reality. Sadhna, in the earlier stages, brings in transformation of mind and body, and hence in the frequency of your vibrations. This either brings an immediate response from nature or ultimately manifests as a miracle.

A word about the three ingredients of meditation:

Breath

Breath is a vital life force. For a healthy living, correct breathing is necessary. Watch a sleeping dog. Its stomach expands with inhalation of breath and goes in with exhalation of breath. The same should be the case with humans. To breathe correctly, let the stomach expand with inhalation and contract with exhalation.

Prana

Prana is that part of breath which consists of cosmic energy. Regulation of Prana helps to balance the energy nodules, called "chakras", in the body. There are seven chakras in our body, situated along the spine. They need to be in balance in order for the energy to flow in in the desired way.

Kriya

Kriyas are of various types. They are a combination of Prana and physical exercises; they tone up the body and mind complex, as well as relax and purify them.

The Art of Living's Sudarshan kriya and the Isha Foundation's Inner Engineering have caught the fancy of young and the old alike.

Affirmation

Affirmation is very popular among the educated youth.

Affirmation is a part of psycho-suggestion. Thought is a powerful energy tool and can convert itself into reality. Hence, empowering the thoughts with positive affirmation leads to actualization. For example, when you wake up from sleep, if you affirm to yourself a healthy life — Today my day will be good; I am happy; I experience joy and happiness — you are actually self-hypnotizing yourself into believing that you, indeed, are happy. The fact is, your subconscious mind absorbs these thoughts. This thought energy will create happiness at some later stage, and joy and happiness will materialize, not in any way from heaven but from your own mind, from your own self. Remember you are the source and you the receiver.

Creative visualization

Sit in a relaxed position. Empty your mind of thoughts. Concentrate on the image you wish to be. Practise this for ten minutes every day. Affirm this image to your subconscious mind and the affirmation will manifest sooner or later in life.

The time between creative visualization and manifestation will vary according to your intensity of purpose. Creative visualization is a slow process. It needs a clear mind and a clear imagination. It is said that once you master this "art" you can even see a person's aura and its colours.

A word of caution to everyone — the manifestation of creative visualization has its negative aspects too. A negative thought is subject to multiplier effect and the real image bounces back with a bang! However, we shall skip this part, bearing in mind the basic principle of Swami Vivekananda, "Be good, Do well."

Meditation

Meditation is all about integrating the mind, and this integration comes through relaxation of the physical body, cleansing of breath—purifying it, and silence within and without.

Based on these three components of meditation, new offbeat techniques have evolved, for example, Osho's Dynamic meditation, Brahma Kumari's "point of light" meditation, and Nahn Nich Tinh's "Psycho-suggestion" meditation. . .

Contemplation and concentration are an important part of mind control and hence of meditation. You may contemplate on a holy picture or a piece of art, or a tree or a flower or concentrate on a candle flame.

Concentration is a focused mind which absorbs all your faculties, senses or energies to an object. Some meditation techniques begin with rituals of lighting a lamp because light plays vital role in the whole process of rejuvenation. In fact some techniques ask you to concentrate on a point of light, or to focus on a candle flame and then take it inward and meditate on it. Some holy men suggest symbols such as the blue lotus or violet light or lingam, varying with individual personality. Concentration on blue lotus is popular as it is easy—we are familiar with lotus flower. Concentration on an inside of a flame is also common, as every household is familiar with Deepawali and the lit candle or wick of a lamp.

For an artist, be a painter or a dancer or a musician, the art itself is meditation as it fully involves their being.
Note: In the initial stage, it is better to take support of recorded meditation. Any mistake in Pranayam can have an opposite effect. Recordings of all the old and new techniques of meditation are available online. You may have your pick.

Affirmation prayer
Among the youth, the prayer of affirmation is very popular. For example, following is the healing affirmation: "Day by day, in every way, I shall get better and better."
"I hereby forgive each and every living soul who has caused me injury, insult, pain, harm, disharmony, and problems. I also pledge to release all the hurt that I have experienced.

O Supreme Being, I humbly beg your forgiveness for all my mistakes and misdemeanours. I am now at peace and brimming with love. My body and soul are becoming healthier and healthier, every day, in every way."

The above prayer should be offered at least five times a day.

Chanting

Another type of meditation extremely popular with the youth, especially those in high pressure jobs, is the Buddhist chant *Range ke ho namoh*. This chant is mostly done in a group. Soka Gakkai International Group (initiated by Ikeda) has spread throughout the world and has become a support system in times of individual crisis. The group meets once a week to chant the Buddhist Mantra and share their experiences of the benefits received from this chant. The group has a well-defined structure of leadership, which guides the group activities.

Sadhna and Past Karma

Most of human suffering arises from the past Karmas.

People are always eager to cancel out their Karmas and avoid bearing pain. They take shelter with a holy person or run to an astrologer or to a Pandit or a clairvoyant or to have reading done from Brighu Shastra written on palm leaves.

As it is said, stones cannot cut your Karmas. Saints can help you in the sense they can help you in *dissolving* your Karmas.

To dissolve the past Karmas, you have to undertake different type of Sadhna, along with the above meditation. In addition, do a good deed every day. Offer a prayer of forgiveness. Do good to those who have hurt you. And thank God for whatever you are, in whatever circumstances you are, wherever you are. Gratitude is an important component of life as it fills you with compassion and love for all beings.

Crystal Comments

The solution to all your problems lies in practice of simple Sadhna.

Mantra Power Compared to Siddhi Power

Siddhis are paranormal, extraordinary, super powers. Siddhis are acquired through mantra and tantra. According to Swami Vishnu Devananda, "A mantra is mystical energy encased in a sound structure. Every mantra contains within its vibrations a certain power. The mantra is so recited as to create vibrations which would empower body, mind, and the spirit. Various mantras have been constructed by our ancient rishis, through combining of sounds that they purify the breath; strengthen the physical, mental, and emotional state of being."

The common mantras in the Hinduism are Om; Beej mantras of Rum, Hum, Yum, etc.; Gayatri mantra; and Mrityunjai mantra. Other regions across the globe also have their "holy name or word". For example, the resonance and the sound effects of Om are similar to that of "Allah O' Akbar". Similarly, parallel mantras are found in the Zoroastrian Gathas. Tibetans and Buddhists have a mantra for everything.

Late Appa Sahib Pant, in his book, *A Moment in Time*, writes how the thunder loaded clouds were stopped from raining in Bhutan through the recitation of mantras, so that he (Appa Sahib Pant) and his family could cross the valley to reach the nearest Indian town.

Nearer home, we have the musician Tansen, of Akbar's nine jewels, who could light a lamp through Raag Deepak and make the sky pour rain through Raag Malhar. The sound of these Ragaas is so powerful that it can transform itself into the desired energy.

Occult Powers: Siddhis and Mantras

Mantras have to be combined with tantra to bestow occult powers. "Tantra" means technique and these techniques are acquired through the vigorous practise of Hath Yoga.

Siddhis are a science. They are the science of superhumans. Patanjali, who is believed to be Shiva Shakti, has described in detail, through Sanskrit slokas, the various powers which can be acquired through various practices. It is like a software for human computers. Each siddhi is like a computer app (application). You click a particular application and create your other double, treble, even multiple self, just the way your app works and produces the results on a computer or mobile phone screen.

There are 3 categories of Siddhis, consisting of more than 120 different types. Known to lay persons are the following Siddhis:

1. Ability to reduce or expand the physical body. (In the case of Vijaya, the sadhu who produced the jasmine flower for her was unusually tall.)
2. Ability to materialize physical objects as in the case of Swami Vivekananda's encounter with the yogi.
3. Ability to enter the consciousness of another human being.
4. Ability to ether double. (The ability to duplicate themselves and appear elsewhere.)
5. Ability to see the aura of a person.
6. Ability to touch the pulse and know of past, present, and future life of a person.
7. Ability to visit (fly) to other planets.
8. Ability to see poltergeist and use poltergeist to one's benefit.
9. Ability to walk on water and fire.

There are many more Siddhis that a lay person may encounter in various walks of life.

Some of the Siddhis travel through birth. Simply speaking, some people are gifted with Siddhis. Others acquire them through yoga and mantra recitation, that is, through sadhna.

Secret Yoga Sutras of Patanjali

a. "Inter-penetrating the physical plane, there are several super physical planes of progressively increasing subtlety. Patanjali says, knowledge of the small, the hidden, or the distant is acquired by directing the light of super physical faculty." Just as one can see distant objects in the sky by looking through a telescope, or can see the inside of a human body through an X-ray, in the same way, by opening up certain "super" faculties, with the help of "source consciousness", one can perform what the lay person calls "miracles". Humans have tremendous inner faculties, which are dormant because of the over-activity of the outer faculties of various sense organs. The super powers or occult powers are acquired by unfolding of the inner faculties.

b. The yogic power to overcome thirst and hunger is acquired by concentration on the gullet — by deactivating the glands for hunger and thirst.

c. L. K. Taimni in *The Science of Yoga* says:

"The mind can enter another's body on relaxation of the cause of bondage and from knowledge of passages. The power of entering the body of another person is a well-known siddhi which occultists sometimes use in their work in the external world." A word of caution. "This should not be confused with the entity entering the body of desire bound disembodied soul which takes temporary possession of the physical body of his victim forcibly in order to satisfy his desire." (For example, the poltergeist at Phaltan or the murder of the doctor's mother in Navrangpura, Ahmedabad.)

The Siddhi of entering the mind of another person is undesirable as it may interfere with that person's Karma or actions of previous births. However noble the intention may be of helping the other person, nevertheless it is a hindrance to the other person's evolution in self-growth, and the purpose of his or her life.

The Crystal Beads

Siddhis are acquired by practising simple yogic kriyas. However, Siddhis are a hindrance to spiritual progress. It is all very simple. What you send out, comes back to you. Siddhis used for selfish purpose bounce back, doing more harm than good. Siddhis performed even for the benefit of someone create obstacles. The bottom line is, chant mantras, for mantras are more powerful than Siddhis and have no side effects. By chanting mantras, life's fulfilment takes a natural course and in due time your wishes and sleeping desires are fulfilled in the most natural and positive way.

Crystal Songs and Siddhi Stories Narrated by Saints

Story of Sri Ramakrishna

A true seeker does not make use of Siddhis because Siddhis are an obstacle to the spiritual growth. Siddhis make a seeker outward, whereas the goal is to go within and have the vision of the Lord.

> A yogi went to Sri Ramakrishna Paramhans. He said to him, "Do you know how I have come across the Hoogly river?" The saint of Dhakheshneshwar remained quiet. "I have walked on water to reach here," the yogi said and added, "It has taken me eight long years of tapas and practice to be able to do so." The saint smiled and said, "You have taken eight long years

to practise yoga just to cross this river. I do so by paying the boatman five paise. The value of your tapas to practise Hath Yoga for eight years is just equal to five paise."

The yogi can walk on water through levitation of the physical body (non-contact with water). This is a Siddhi — a technique acquired to control the physical body. Yogis acquire this Siddhi in the process of their performing certain kriyas. However Siddhis are not or of little value to humankind.

Sufi Saint Rabia

One day, Rabia was sitting with a few followers outside her house. Hasan came to her and said, "Rabia, you are wasting time doing penance and 'bhakti' for so long. What have you gained? Look at me. I can walk on water. Let's go out and sit on a water stream." Rabia, in her wisdom, replied, "I have no need to do so. A fish can float on water; a fly or an insect can swim in the air. I do not want to be a fish or a fly." Further, Rabia said, "Your power of remaining still on water is the one possessed by fish. My power of flying in the air is possessed by a fly. These abilities are not part of the real Truth — they may become the foundation of Ego, and not of spirituality. These Siddhis are not the Truth. In fact, they are ego boosters and ego is the enemy of all goodness!"

Swami Vivekananda's Views on Siddhis

Swami Vivekanand, in his speech delivered in Los Angeles, California on January 8, 1900, spoke about the "Power of Mind" and its actualization through various practices known to East and West. He narrated his personal experience:

Once I went to test a man who claimed extraordinary powers. I wrote something on a piece of paper, which the man asked me to fold, sign on its back, put it in my pocket, and keep it there till he asked for it again. After a while, he said, "Now think of a word or a sentence from any language you like." I thought of a long sentence in Sanskrit, a language which he was totally ignorant of. "Now take out the piece of paper from your pocket," he said. The Sanskrit sentence was written there!

Reading the Unseen

A trained mind can communicate with another human mind through the symbiotic universal mind.

A lay person, like you and me, need not bother about all these powers. All that we need to know is that mind control is necessary for any kind of success in life. Prayer is power, and Love is God!

8

Mystical Healing

Mystical Therapy

Mystical healing is as old as human civilization on this earth. The only difference is that earlier it was mixed with belief, faith, and myth and so was clouded in mystery. Today, most of these healing techniques are scientifically recorded and proved. The discovery of Krilian photography in 1958, and its subsequent development, made a scientific breakthrough in what came to be called, "alternative medicine". Krilian photography also referred to as "bio-electrography", is now widely used in Astrology, 'Gemmology, Parapsychology, and Reiki all over the world.

As a teenager, I remember, that anyone who contracted jaundice was advised to go, to an old Parsi gentleman living in a far off Mumbai suburb. He, through his mystical chant, used to cure people of their ailment. When my daughter had jaundice, I was advised to take her to a particular temple and get a Tulsi Mala, by wearing which she would be cured. I did not believe in it. But today, with so many scientific proofs available on the vibrations of crystals and sounds of different chants, one feels there is truth in it.

The cynical are bound to question this. But let me tell you, I have known two cases of children who were born with some negative disturbance of past life, and they were challenged in some way or the other. Today these very kids are super kids, thanks to the mystical healing through Reiki and chant-sound therapy.

There are numerous types of mystical healing, now termed sophisticatedly as therapy. The popular ones in India are Reiki, Pranic healing, Pyramid healing, Sound therapy, Gems therapy, Chant therapy, Aroma therapy, and borrowing from the western world, is light therapy.

Light Therapy

Human beings are made of light. This light has different vibrations and voltages in different beings. Every second the human body emanates light which is invisible to human eye. This light energy has a frequency. To heal any ailment, you have to tune this energy to a higher energy and to a specific fine tuning; it is just like tuning in to a particular radio station. Just as in a radio or a T.V. channel, there is a source, a carrier, and a receiver, in the same way, it is you, your higher self and the carrier or the transformer, which is the light. Under this therapy, one builds bridges of light between self and higher self. The rest takes care of itself. The Universe begins to work in your favour. The rhythm of life improves. Everything falls into place.

Human beings are born with certain soul qualities. Through the tool of light, these qualities are explored and brought in tune with the higher self. Everyone will agree that 90 per cent of illness is caused by the condition of the mind. In other words, whenever mind's vibrations are out of synch with your heart and soul vibrations, disease strike. Often the mind vibrations are negative, but our soul vibrations are pure and of a higher frequency. When the gap widens, it creates misunderstandings, despair, depression, and diseases, ranging from physical to neurological ones. To bridge the gap, build bridges of light and remove the cause of disturbances.

This therapy or tool of light is most useful and effective in repairing broken or tarnished relationships and emotional problems. According to the author Launa Huffines, a crusader for "Bridges of Light", this tool is not for one time use. It is to be practised over a period of time, along with the rhythm of life, brought in by deep, slow breathing in a quiet environment.

Reiki

Reiki is a form of spiritual healing. It uses the tool of universal energy to heal body, mind, and the spirit. We may not be the centre of the Universe, but we are surely a part of the Universe. There is a definite connection between individual energies and the Universal energy.

This truth has existed in India since time immemorial. It was a Japanese by name of Mr. Mikao Usai who revived this mystical Tibetan system of "Energy Medicine" in the late 19th century. The name Reiki is Japanese — Rei - Universal, Ki - energy. Reiki is a flow of energy, which is channelled through the "attuned" energy channel of the human body to heal and re-balance the energy levels. The most beautiful part of Reiki is that "once you are balanced inside, life will fall into its own place."

Our physical body, thoughts, and emotions are composed of life force, namely, energy, which operates at different frequencies in different people. Reiki is able to raise this life force energy and correct it by exposing it to higher vibratory frequency of the universal energy, which is pure and light.

At Stanford University in the USA, a research project was undertaken to see the effects of Reiki on cancer. It is believed that most of our diseases are emotion related. By restoring the chakra balance, many dreadful diseases can be overcome.

I had two experiences with learning of Reiki.

> The first experience was while we were being attuned to the universal energy at a class in Sadhu Vaswani Mission, half of the attendees vomited. The reason given was that for many persons, Reiki works as psychotherapy. The negative emotions imbibed in early childhood and suppressed in adulthood had to be rejected and released to make way for positive energy.

> The second experience is that distant Reiki works best if you are connected with the Reiki Master. I do not know the reason. Perhaps when working on Reiki face to face, other emotions and doubts on both the sides become obstructions and come in the way of healing.

Reiki symbols

Reiki gives best results when combined with attitude of gratitude. Positive affirmations help in every type of mystical healing!

Dr. Arjun, a well-known Diabolist from Bengaluru, is a seeker who travels the Himalayas extensively. On one of his trips he met a French woman, also a seeker. She said she could read sound—not only see sound, but also read it. She had this extra perception! Her goal was to use her skill for curing diseases.

Sound therapy is also all about vibrations and their frequency. Sound therapy includes, in terms of vibrations, electro-crystal therapy, Radionics and, health Kinesiology.

In olden days, singing was common. Women, while cleaning or cooking or doing their daily chores, would hum a tune or sing a song. This has calming effect on their nerves. Nowadays, crooning or humming is out. It is the radio or the mobile that sings, leaving little space for the individual to sing.

The esoteric schools of India, Tibet, Greece, and Egypt had the knowledge of curative powers of sound. Pythagoras has written that mathematics of music can be worked out so as to control the mind, the breath, and also the purification of a person.

In 1920, a German scientist Hans Kayser, and a Swiss scientist Dr. Hans Jenny, experimented with music on plants and metals, by using different sound frequencies. They discovered that the plants grew much better and faster with certain notes of music. Jonathan Goldman, a pioneer of sound therapy, was of the opinion that diseases in the body were caused by out of tune vibrations. A disease could be cured by restoring the harmonic balance in the body.

Under sound therapy, we have Om therapy, Chant therapy, Music therapy and, of course, the Humming Therapy, etc.

You may have heard the saying—hum yourself to happiness. Humming is the best way to relax nerves. Any kind of sound which gives you a feeling of expansion and lightness has curative effects.

Healing Rituals

Hug a tree and be healed!
Indigenous people, tribal, gypsy, and others live a natural life. Surrounded by trees, water, earth, and sun, they seek energy and healing energy in their natural environment. Their native wisdom, based on instinct and intuition, helped them to evolve the rituals which help in healing.

Ritual related to trees: Worship the tree in reverence, taking it to be a symbol of the Creative Universe. A tree is truly a Shiva. And so it becomes a deity worthy of worship. What makes a tree Shiva? It's self-creating energy. A tree creates its own seed, and from that seed it is born again. Even western mystic poets recognized this truth. Robert Ernest Hume confirms it when he writes:

> A tree, when felled, grows up
> From the root, more new again
> A mortal when cut down by death
> From what root does he grow up?

A tree's birth is a lesson in the self-sacrifice it under takes. The seed completely merges with the earth; it annihilates itself for the benefit of the world. And one seed produces hundreds of seeds, all imbued with the self-creating energy.

A tree has all the spiritual qualities and it confirms to the Law of Abundance. As the saying goes—give nature one seed, and it grows for you plenty of them. A tree is the beautiful example of Law of Forgiveness—throw a stone at a tree and it rewards you with fruits. A tree has positive energy—it provides you continuously with fresh energy. Hug a tree in reverence and you can draw abundant positive spiritual healing energy.

Symbol Worship

Creating symbols to represent as deities or energy channels is common all over the world. All the "ritualistic" symbols are potent with Shakti and carry healing properties.

A rural ritual, common in many communities worshiping the female deity, is to create the symbol representing the Goddess by draping a coconut with a sari and painting eyes and nose, and putting ornaments on it. This is placed on a *kalash* and worshipped by glorifying it and offering sacrifice by way of observing fast on that day. Such a symbol represents Mother, and so the person worshiping it actually does creative visualization, glorifying it, and in the process acquires the qualities of love. It is believed that in this ritual a golden light flows from the heart, which carries healing qualities.

Yogic Kriyas like Surya Namaskar are loaded with healing. The Sufi twirl dance is also a Yogic Kriya as it is performed after putting the chakras in balance. The ecstatic dance, which puts the Sufi in a trance, is the result of balance in energy and rhythm in body, all of which are healing.

Dance, Dream, and be healed!

9
Mystical Connect

Miracles of Connecting

Dialogue with destiny!
From one life to another, the tunnel is very small. At the end of the tunnel is light or spheres of light. One ascends the spheres of light according to one's actions, deeds, and selfless surrender to Dharma.

Saints often connect with the invisible spheres and seek answers to mysteries of life. In one such adventure in the unseen world, Sadhu Vaswani connected with his invisible helper, the Guardian Angel.

Sadhu Vaswani — a mystic, a poet, and a giant intellectual — was also the Principal of three prestigious colleges of undivided India. Founder of Mira Movement in education, with the focus on Atma Vidya, he was an educationist, a social pioneer, and a feminist, who chose to be an Illahi Fakir, following the path of selfless service. He was a saint par excellence. He, too, had his Guardian Angel.

While searching for matter on the museum, now named as Darshan, which depicts the life of Sadhu Vaswani, I read many interesting facts about his life. The most fascinating, perhaps, was his conversation with his Guardian Angel. He has mentioned this conversation with the Invisible Angel in one of his memoirs, written in Sindhi. Here is the English translation of that fascinating passage:

> I found my Guru in physical form in a young brahamcharya of Bengal, Sri Promotholal Sen of Kolkata. But outside this material frame, that is, the temporal world, in the spiritual sphere, I found a Guru with the grace of God. I call him Master or Gurudev. From time to time, the Master, in his benevolence, sends me messages. These messages come when I am in tune with him. One night, after 12 o' clock, as I sat in silence in communion with my Master, I asked him some questions. He answered them through a medium.

I place before you that dialogue which I heard in silence, in the depth of the night. Those who want to believe, may believe; those who are sceptical have a right to reject it. I request the readers to give a sincere thought to these conversations.

Question

Master, give me a teaching in the silence of the night.

Answer

Come Nuri, you have fallen in love with Nama, so renounce the world and identify yourself with Bhakti.

Hence mould some devotees for the sacred feet of Krishna or Christ.

For the sake of Nama, everyone should surrender to Nama.

Question

Kindly tell me who you are, and what is your work in the other (ether) sphere of life?

Answer

I am an Angel. By the grace and blessings of Krishna or Christ, I have reached this state of bliss. My job is to look after Nuri, take care of his work on the earth plane, and to heed the call of any human being in need of me or who is facing a crisis.

Question

What kind of life were you living before you reached angelhood? Kindly describe it.

Answer

I had taken birth in another world (plane). Even there, my time was spent in the service of others. I also went ecstatic with Nama Jap. When I died, I went to the Stage 3. I understood, then, that this or that world is only a play of Maya.

One day I saw the light of Krishna or Christ and I experienced that radiance for many years. What a light!

Question

Do you have a message for my Satsangis?

Answer

Satsangis cannot hear my voice, they will be able to hear your voice. You explain to them this, that they should spend more and more time in silence and follow the voice of conscience. In worldly affairs, in their mundane dealings, they should bear witness to their Guru and live a life of Dharma.

Question

How many stages are there in the spiritual sphere?

Answer

The number of stages varies from religion to religion. For example, while Hinduism suggests seven stages, the western sacred scriptures suggest up to nine stages.

Question

Where does the guidance come from?

Answer

By the grace of God, one moves from one sphere to another. Every sphere has a Guardian Angel. But the great guidance comes from the sphere of Super Consciousness.

I have earned blessings, for I serve the great fakirs and dervishes. That humble service has brought me this divine grace.

Translated from Sindhi writings of Sadhu Vaswani

Saints connect themselves with the Divine World during the deep meditation in the night between 12 o' clock and 3 o' clock in the morning. Saints, or those on the spiritual path, connect with their devotees just before the Brahma Mahurat and answer the questions during the Brahma Mahurat period. Hence the common belief that dreams at the time of dawn come true. They materialize as they are the guidance from the above. They also connect you, during this period, with the people you love dearly.

Saints and the Dreams

A true saint answers the "call of distress" by appearing in a dream.

The saints have a powerful spiritual radar system. At midnight, when they sit in meditation, they raise their consciousness high, till it touches the Supreme Divine Consciousness which is Universal. There they get connected with the "calls" and receive them. They answer them according to the Divine Will or according to the guidance of their guide in the Spirit World.

The Crystal Candle

There are many worlds. Humans are unable to see the other worlds because they are wrapped up in veils of Maya. With sadhna and prayer, one can live a life of awareness and, hence, of joy and peace. The best time to meditate and pray is early morning, when the mind-body complex is fresh and receptive – earlier the better.

A Beautiful Life after Life

According to Hindu philosophy, there are seven stages or spheres of life after Death.

In another incident, Sadhu Vaswani connected with the spirit called Yama Raj, the Shakti which rules death or the tunnel that connects life here and the life there in the ether, invisible world. Sadhu T. L. Vaswani also had a conversation with the Invisible.

I quote a few sentences of the lyrical conversation. The dialogue is a revelation. It is the voice of wisdom.

Sadhu Vaswani: Yama of the Dark Face!
              Why must thou take me now?
              Take me from the dear ones?
              Take me from myself?

Yama: Child! Thou has not seen thyself;
              The atman dieth not, nor is killed;
              'Tis the form, the sthula sharir dieth;
              The sutra, the thread of life remains.

Sadhu Vaswani: The earth is rich in colour and laughter,
              But in thy presence, Yama,
              I feel like a thin shrunken, pale,
              Sent out to wander in vacant space.

Yama: The highest human happiness,
              No better is than soap bubble!
              Thy happiness, child, is not here,
              But in the Mansions whence thou comest.

Sadhu Vaswani: But the sea seems rough!

Yama: Beyond it are the angels,
              The Devas in radiance clothed
              Waiting on the harbour
              To greet thee home.

Sadhu Vaswani:

The other side is not lonely, for the Great Ones are active there.

But to know the mystery of death, you must be in tune with the heart-beats of life.

For life is the river that flows on, until it enters into the greater life that man calls death,

Even as the Indus flows on, until it enters into the Great Indian Ocean.

The Crystal Window

Fear not death, for it is a window to a better and a more beautiful world. Live today, free and joyfully, for tomorrow is the promise of great hope!

Live in this world, free, without self-imposed walls. Dissolve the invisible walls in the mind by purification through various sadhna, like early morning mantra jaap, a holy prayer, by Buddhist chants, or by purifying breath through Om therapy.

Miracles or Premonitions: Death Is Light

Nothing is born, nothing is dead;
'Tis his fancy to dust we are laid,
For joy to be, for sorrow made!

Death is a mystery. It is also some light. Perhaps the light of the helpers beyond.

> A friend had a strange experience. Five hours before her mother-in-law died, she saw a beam of light, which swept across the room. For a moment she thought it was a hallucination. Then she confirmed it with her husband, who was sitting next to her. Sceptical, they thought that their landlord, who had come down from Rishikesh, had come with his torchlight as he had expressed his wish to sleep, in the backyard under the neem tree. After half an hour, the landlord knocked on the wicket gate and flashing his yellow torchlight enquired whether they were at home.
>
> "But you came in half an hour ago, didn't you?" They asked, surprised. "No," he replied emphatically, "I have just come and I am still standing at the wicket gate." That night, at 4 o' clock, they got a phone call that the mother-in-law was no more.

The same friend had a similar experience when her mother died. At that time she was with her in Nanavati hospital in Mumbai. While looking out of the window, waiting for her husband to come and relieve her from the hospital duty, she saw the same beam of light. At first she dismissed it as a light from the airport at Santa Cruz or the mini airport at Juhu nearby.

But the light was a thin, blue, rotating beam. It was different from a usual light. Bearing witness to the beautiful light, death arrived after three hours. And as the four angels, described by her mother, took her away, there was a radiant glow on her face.

"My mother had never looked so beautiful as then," she confided later.

Why this radiance? Is death a freedom that beholds light? To which the Master replied, "When you die, you drink the waters of the River of Silence. And drinking in silence and coming to the other side, you glimpse the light and your soul bursts into a song of joy!"

If death is so beautiful, then why do we fear it?
We should fear life and not death!

Premonition 1

Bharat's grandfather, Raghavji, called his family to the *baithak*. It was noon, and summer time.

"Today, we shall eat our dinner early," he said.

"Grandpa, we are Jains. We eat our dinner early," said Bharat.

"I mean, today we shall eat dinner at 4 o'clock instead of 6 o'clock. So please, ladies of the house, go and prepare the evening meal," he said and retired to his room.

The family of three generations quietly went to do his bidding. No one had the courage to ask why. Why this new schedule?

As Gujarati Jains, they ate their lunch at 11 o'clock in the morning and their dinner at 6.30 (much before the sunset) in the evening. But that day, Grandfather had instructed the family to finish their dinner early and relax in the evening.

The family did not question his decision. At 4 o'clock sharp, the family sat down on the kitchen floor and had their meal. By 5 o'clock the kitchen was washed and cleaned. At 6 o'clock Raghavji breathed his last.

"He knew he would be gone at 6 o'clock. He did not wish his family to remain hungry for twenty four hours," said Raghavji's wife.

Raghavji knew his exact time of death. The funeral rites and death ceremonies in India last a long time, during which the family does not take cooked food.

Premonition 2

Intuition or premonition can be developed by practising simple meditation—sadhna. Miss. Sushma Padnekar of Goa has said in one of the books, *Awakening Spiritual Emotions*, that there is power in chanting God's name. By prayer, meditation, and Guru's grace, you are spiritually awakened. This is what she says:

> I would get a premonition about an impending illness or death in the village. When in Class X, about five days before the death of my father, I knew that he would experience severe distress and die, and this is exactly what happened.

This story is a hundred years old. It happened in a place called Bijapur in Karnataka. This is just one story of premonition of death. There are many such stories. Strangely enough, the recorded ones all belong to the same period of time—more than a hundred years ago from now, that is, in the nineteenth century. During those times, people were less materialistic and followed the spiritual practices of their faith. This made them intuitive and perceptive.

Premonitions of Death

Long ago, people would get the premonition of their death. Lay persons could sense that their time was up. The Brahmins, with their purified mind, could see death. Those who can read the aura also can predict death by discerning the quality and the colour of the aura.

Saints, for sure, know when they are going to die or leave their body. Some even write down the time and date of their death. Just as the ancient communities like the Red Indians knew the exact time of an impending storm, and the dogs start barking at death signals, in the same way it is said that we can know our death.

There are many myths and legends about the prediction of death. Certain dreams indicate death. Certain signs indicate death. It is said, if you recite Jap sahib every day without a break, you can know the time of leaving this world!

Swami Ramakrishna Parmahans

> Swami Ramakrishna was a realized soul. He came to know of his death three days in advance. This was communicated to his consort, Sri Sharda Devi Ma. Naturally, she cried, as she did not wish to be a widow. Seeing her weep, the Master, Swami Ramakrishna, said to her:
>
> "Why do you cry? Because the one who is, is not going to die. Did you love this physical body known as me or do you love the one who is me?"
>
> Sharda replied, "I loved the one who is." Ramakrishna said, "Then drop the worry. Then, when he who is and does not die, do not break your bangles as a widow."
>
> Perhaps Sharda Ma was the only widow of her times in Bengal, who did not break her bangles on becoming a widow.

At the passing away of Sri Ramakrishna, everyone else cried and wept but Sharda Ma maintained her calm. She did not break her bangles. She remained the same as she always was. She said, "One who has died was not there in the first place, and the one who was there, still is." Whenever somebody asked she would say, "That body had become worn and torn, he has only changed clothes."

Sadhu T. L. Vaswani

Sadhu T. L. Vaswani (1879-1966) was a scholarly saint, and a pioneer of women's education. He is the founder of Mira Movement in education, inculcating Brahm Vidya and Rishi Culture. His core philosophy was twofold — Love and Give.

Three days before he left this shore, he asked for his clothes. Keeping a change of clothes, he distributed the remaining among the poor. He wrote his own funeral song, "Khuda Hafiz, Khudha Hafiz" in Sindhi, before he moved on to the golden shore!

Whenever the enlightened souls move from this world to the other, they are escorted by angels of light. Sometimes these beams of light become visible to some people.

The Crystal Chime Rings

Death is a light. Death is positive. Death is not something negative and to be feared. Death is a natural phenomenon which transports us to a new sphere of life.

His Love for His Wife: She Visited Him Every Night

The Unseen writes and speaks
His wife wrote to him every night
What is sunset here, is sunrise there!

I met him at the inauguration of the library wing of the College. He was an old, saintly man and was sitting and vacantly looking into space.

"Can you see the things beyond space?" I asked.

"I can hear, and I can read," he replied.

He invited my daughter and me to his house.

It was the time of twilight, gathering dusk. We were welcomed by the loud bark of his ferocious dog.

"Everything here looks and feels eerie," said my daughter.

As we entered the house, which was on the outskirts of Pune, my daughter said, "I feel a dead body is buried here."

True enough, the ashes of the cremated dead body of his wife were buried by the side of the living room.

Before I could ask anything, he said, "I loved my wife so much that I had to bury her here." My shock and surprise were all mixed together. I was a non-believer, and did not believe in formal religious ceremonies.

After we settled down he began his story:

> My wife, Veena, left her physical body on Thursday, 23-2-1967 at 2.30 a.m. Not believing in any ceremony, I did not call any Brahmin—the body was simply taken to the cremation ground and everybody who came was informed that there would be no third day or eleventh day ceremony, as Hindus generally observe these days.
>
> I brought her ashes home as I had a vision about 13 years ago that my Veena had left me and, after the cremation, her ashes were brought home and her samadhi had been constructed. This vision of mine was narrated to her in my letter dated 8-2-1954, when we were in Jaipur for a holiday.
>
> On 15-3-1967, Wednesday, that is, after 21 days, I saw her standing on the last step of the staircase. At that time I was having dinner with my sister. I was not frightened and mentally asked her to come over. She went to the terrace and then to her bedroom.
>
> A friend of hers, Miss. Katy Engineer, told me to attend the Sunday meeting where her friends met and called spirits. I thought there was no harm in going. So on Sunday, 19-3-1967, I attended the meeting at 10 a.m. As it was a very new thing for me, I sat quietly on one of the chairs. The medium called his guide and requested him to call Veena. When she came, I asked some questions mentally about her meeting with me

and her wearing a dress on 18-3-1967. She gave the correct replies and I was so moved that I could not put any more questions to her.

After that, I took interest in the subject, and we used to meet and speak mentally.

Earlier, we used to talk mentally, but now we use automatic writing. When she writes, though through my hands, I feel that my hands are not under my control.

Every night I select the saris for her and she meets me in the morning in that sari. Many times I forget, but she reminds me by wearing the same sari which I chose the previous night. Here are the details of our conversation:

P.: Do you remember the name of the doctor and the hospital?

Veena: Dr. Desai at Cancer Hospital.

P.: Do you know I feel happy when you are with me and I feel your presence everywhere.

Veena: We can't be separated under any circumstances. By God, we both were attached in such a way that no one can separate us. Pray to God.

P.: But you know, I do not pray.

Veena: But I pray.

P.: Do you know, when I go to cinema, I purchase two tickets — the second one for you? Which pictures have you seen with me?

Veena: Yes, I was with you at Asra, Mila, Gaban, Shakespeare Walla.

On 13-6-1967, Tuesday, morning, I was sitting alone in my office. Veena was sitting in the chair next to me. I was upset due to office affairs. She took me far away to a desert, my first occasion of astral travelling. She showed me a big caravan, moving silently and steadily, in the same direction. Suddenly, I saw a disturbance in the caravan. All the camels were scattered. She took me further and showed me the condition of scattered animals. All had become victims of vultures. She gave me a clear vision of a steady caravan and a scattered one. Then, she told me to apply this in the administration of my office. I was silent in response.

On 20-6-1967, Tuesday, at 4 a.m. she gave me the following message: "I will guide you. You are being guarded. Be careful, my Pritam. I am with you. Keep quiet, that is good. Don't get excited. There is too much work ahead."

On 3-7-1967, Monday, at 6 p.m., I had the second sitting with Mr. Rishi, the medium. Veena's friend was writing the message given by her. "I am Veena. I am happy now. I always come with you wherever you go, just to keep you in normal mind. I try to inspire you. After I left my body, I was moving around my body trying to re-enter it, but I failed. I was sorry that you were sad. Two persons were present. They took me in the fourth plane first. I was resting. I came to the fifth plane and began to pray to God. After some days, my mind was steady. I met my guide. He gave me lessons on how to meditate, how to pray and how to help my dear ones. Since then I have used to this world. My guide told me not be restless, but to help and guide your husband. He, the guide, is an advanced soul. We call him 'Master'."

On 4-7-1967, Tuesday, at 5 a.m., Veena gave me the following message:

"I am your Veena. Yes, I have a separate guide. I communicate with you through thoughts and convey them to your head. It is my brain that is thinking while you write these messages. Yesterday, I told you that I called my guide 'Master'. Yes, he is a very big personality. Yes, Sri Ramakrishna is my Master. You also call him Master. At his feet I learn everything. He is the noblest of all. With his guidance, I move freely. Do you feel lonely now? You know, I always sleep with you. In every walk of yours, I am with you. You are blessed by my Master. In appearance, you never pray, but in your heart of hearts, you are praying. But you never show it. During my sickness, you were calling the Master, you were calling Swami Parmanand Chidakashi. Yes, I have met him also. His blessings are on you. I had great faith in you. I only believed in you. I still have faith in you, my Pritam, and that is why you are my light. After few minutes I have to go — it is now 5.30 a.m., my Pritam — Yours, Veena."

On 12-8-1967, Saturday, I got up earlier than usual. My Veena came and touched my face. I inquired whether message can be written without my hand. Veena gave me the following message:

"I am your Veena. Yes, my Pritam, these are all wonders. But we do not do such things. This is a deep matter. Not to worry, at present. My Pritam, you had an experience. Have a normal life. Yes, you can see and hear as two souls. My Gul, the way we are moving is right. I am going. I have some duty to do. It is 5 a.m. Yours, Veena."

12-8-1967, Saturday evening, she gave me the following message: "I am your Veena. Sadhna or meditation has to be done in a very quiet place. The time after midnight, say 3 or 4 a.m., is the best time for meditation. Control your breathing. By controlling your breathing, you can control your whole boy. Controlled breathing means deep breathing. Have practice and you will feel different. When you come to that stage, you will feel complete electrification of your body. At that time, try to prolong that period and say 'Om'. It is enough to simply chant Om."

On 15-6-1980, Sunday, I was reading *The Gospel of Sri Ramakrishna*. On page 186, our Master says: "The practise of discipline is absolutely necessary. Why shouldn't a man succeed if he practises sadhna? But he does not have to work hard if he has real faith in his Guru's words . . ."

While reading *The Gospel of Sri Ramakrishna* on 15-5-1982, I came across the following instructions given to his devotees on page 550: "What need of rituals has a man, what need of devotions, any more, if he respects the Mother's name at three holy hours? The sandhya merges in Gayatri, the Gayatri in Om. A man is firmly established in spiritual life when he goes in samadhi by uttering 'Om' only once. To read a great many scriptures is not necessary. It is much better to pray to God in solitude."

16-9-1983, at 4.30 a.m., I was reading *The Gospel of Sri Ramakrishna*, page 590. Our Master says to his devotees: "**By siddhi, I mean the attainment of the spiritual goal and not one of the eight occult powers. About occult powers, Sri Krishna said to Arjun: 'Friend, if you find anyone who has acquired even one of the eight powers, then know for certain he will not realize me, for powers surely beget pride and God cannot be realized if there is slightest trace of pride."**

On 30-8-85, while reading the book *Lenin Talks to America* by Savva Dangulov, I came to know more about Lenin than what my Veena told me about him. In Lenin's message of 1-9-1967, he talks about purity of thought and higher thinking and the following tallies with his message:

"Truth is good for the soul — A diplomacy that can win over everything that is best on the other side, everything that is honest and effective! We shall win them over by the truth, our truth! For it is we who possess the truth! And what is a man not capable of when the truth is on his side? And men will come to us in the end, for honesty, for rationality, for a good life, for happiness. Man has grown up! He understands that only our truth can make him happy."

28-6-1986, Tuesday 4 a.m. I was reading *The Gospel of Sri Ramakrishna*. On page 280 our Master Sri Ramakrishna says: "It is enough to chant simply Om. . . . How long should a man practise such devotion as the sandhya? As long as he does not feel a thrill in his body and shed tears of joy while repeating the name of Rama and Hari."

On 16-9-1993, at 4.30 a.m. I was reading *The Gospel of Sri Ramakrishna*. On page 590 our Master says: "No one put a limit to spiritual experience. If you refer to one experience, there is another beyond that and still another and so on."

From time to time, I tried to verify the facts by reading the original instructions from the Gospel of Sri Ramakrishna.

I verified Veena's message regarding Lenin by reading about Lenin.

Pritam received maximum messages of Ramakrishna Paramahansa from Veena through auto-writing from 1967 to 1987; later the messages were from her master of higher region. Pritam verified the Ramakrishna Paramhansa's messages delivered by Veena by studying the *Gospel of Sri Ramakrishna Paramahansa*. The verification took place at different times as Pritam could not read the Gospel at a stretch.

True love is between two souls. It can communicate anywhere in the Universe. It is this love—the Soul Love—which is pure and non-karmic. Veena had a definite purpose in communicating the messages from the other world, namely, to evoke love to the divine, to transform an atheist into a believer.

What a beautiful and noble idea!

(The message of Lenin was given on 1-9-1967. On 3-3-1968, *The Times of India* gave a big news, with the heading "World Red Unity Crumbling Warns Hungary.")

The Unseen's True Love

Pritam and Veena's story continues!

Love is the rebirth of human soul,
A heaven lit by another shore.

15-10-1967, Sunday (Poona): I got up at 4 a.m. and she gave me the following message:

"My Pritam, I am your Veena. We belong to the whole Universe. We do not belong to an individual country. We have some connection with the land of birth, that is why we have some connection with individual who is known to us and loved by us. We meet the people of other lands also, if we were known to them or we go through somebody who is known to us here. Yours Veena."

On 21-10-1967 she said: "*Mere* Pritam, I am your Veena. Slowly and gradually bring me within your magnetic field. That is your success. My Pritam, **there are many circles, pass from** these small circles and be within the big circle. That is your destination. That is a stage of eternal happiness."

I did not understand the circles indication. As she left at 5.40 a.m., I came out in the open yard. As I was strolling and looking up in the sky at the moon, with nature around me, my body was being charged by energy, bit by bit. When it was fully charged, tears were rolling down my cheeks. There are no words to describe the state in which I was. The tears were not of sadness but of joy – real happiness. She had lifted me from the dustbin. There were no words to express myself. I was floating in happiness.

This message had come from Veena in 1967; but Pritam found the same message in the Gospel of Sri Ramakrishna in 1980. This message is very important for humankind, as it contains the entire philosophy of the Adwaitiva – I am that or what comes from the Source returns to the Source, having progressed or grown bigger and bigger in that process!

On 16-9-1980, I was reading *The Gospel of Sri Ramakrishna*. I understood the meaning of the message given by my dear Veena earlier when she was drawing a circle and then one big circle. She was making the big circle thicker. There is a deep meaning in the circles drawn by her, as I learnt from Swami Vivekanand.

"In this world, there are some circles into which human beings are drawn in by their weaknesses. In other circles, they get realization. These circles are interconnected. When a person is in the circle of temptation, and if he or she is strong enough, they step in the circle of realization." So, an individual is passing through circles. If they are a weak personality, they remain within the circle of temptations, fall and are finished. Once they pass through all these small circles, they come within the bigger circle, which is the strongest one, where they get self-realization, that is, being one with Him.

Swami Vivekananda has beautifully explained the meaning of small circle and big circle in the book *Patanjali Yoga Sutra*. He writes: "Every motion is in a circle. If you could take up a stone, and project it into space, and then live long enough, that stone would come back exactly to your hand. A straight line, infinitely projected, must end in a circle."

Before the year 1967 when Veena passed away, I did not know about sadhna or meditation. I was a complete non-believer, but she, by and by, lifted me up through her messages — sometimes with love, sometimes by hitting me hard, and sometimes by inducing me by showing the wonders in the astral world.

Practically all her messages tally with the messages of Sri Ramakrishna. It clearly shows that she is under the guidance of the great, heavenly soul. Her progress in astral world has really inspired me and that is why I have got full faith in her. I never harbour any doubts now. She has guided me and she will guide me up to the end.

When I started writing this diary, I wrote, "Believe it or not, but it is a fact." From the above narration of our Master, it is clear that my Veena used to come and give me instructions which tally with instructions of our Master, Sri Ramakrishna. I started reading *The Gospel of Sri Ramakrishna* after 30-12-1974. I purchased the book in Calcutta.

Being a Godless man, but after verification of all facts, I have come to the conclusion that my Veena really acted as my Guide, my light and my Goddess. With all this, how can I disbelieve?

True love lifts you up to a higher self.

The Golden Chime

There are mediums – vehicles – or saints who are working for a higher cause. It is a well-known fact that there are several mediums of Sai Meher Baba working for mitigating human suffering and guiding people in the sphere of work and relationships by lifting them into higher circles of happiness and higher hemispheres of light.

The Night Vigil

The night Vigil was held in a house in a dark lane in Santa Cruz, Mumbai. Monica and I went there at 10 p.m. The "Conductor" was to arrive late as he was coming from Nagar. I had heard a lot about his healing powers. He was tall and hefty, full of laughter, wearing western clothes, branded jeans and a T-shirt. He looked like the guy who went partying all night. But in fact, he was deeply spiritual and in touch with his Master, who gave him the foresight.

> When we entered, we found the crowd had already gathered, the centre lamp was lit and windows closed. A glass filled with lemonade and another filled with rose water was kept at the entrance. Hundreds of joss sticks burned, spreading the flower aroma and the *dhoop* smoke was still in the air. All this was done to purify the air.
>
> There was pin drop silence. Absolute silence. The devotees waited for the silence to seep in; there was a strange peace. Out of the depths of serenity, a sonorous voice rose, higher and higher, to reach a crescendo. The chorus followed. Gradually, everyone's silenced emotions awakened and the dust around the soul was wiped off.
>
> At the break of dawn, we returned home. It is at this place that Monica had her experience. It was as mystical as shattering.
>
> Monica had become a widow at a young age. Like any *pativrata* Hindu woman, she sought to be connected with her husband. It was in one of these sessions that she felt an embrace of a huge man, who pulled and kissed her. The pull was so strong that she fell down. She was transported to another world. When she opened her eyes, she saw the Conductor of the vigil by her side. But it wasn't he who had hugged her and kissed her. It was her husband. She saw him distinctly, the same touch, the same eagerness, the same clothes.
>
> "Who was he?" She asked the Conductor.
>
> "He was your husband," he replied with a smile.

Thereafter, she stopped worrying. She was sure her husband was really connected with her and would guide her when she needed him.

They Remember Their Previous Life

After I was told of my traumatic death in the previous birth, I recollected the stories of reincarnation narrated to me by Swamiji, who had worked with Dr. Ivan Stevenson of Virginia University and had handed me a few original research papers.

Rajul, Who Was Gita

One of the case that was given to me is that of Rajul.

> Rajul Shah was born on August 14, 1960, in Vinchhiya, a small village near Rajkot in Gujarat. After her birth, she lived with her parents at Keshod, the bird sanctuary town of Saurashtra. In March 1963, when Rajul was barely two-and-a-half years old, she went to stay for a while with her grandparents, Mr. and Mrs. V. J. Shah, at Wankaner. Mr. V. J. Shah was then a Consulting Engineer at Wankaner. At that time, many relatives were staying with her grandparents as there was a religious function in town. One of the relatives casually asked Rajul where she had come from. To this the girl replied, "From Junagadh, Aunty." As Rajul was very young, the family did not attach much importance to her answer. But gradually it became evident that Rajul had something to do with Junagadh.
>
> Two years later, in May 1965, Rajul's family went to Rajkot to attend the consecration of the idol of a Tirthanker in a temple. On this occasion, a model of the holy mountain, Sumitshikhar of Bihar, where the Tirthanker had attained Nirvana, had been built. On the model they had shown the steps leading up the mountain. Seeing this, Rajul said to her grandmother, "Grandma, we used to make such a model of Girnar in Junagadh. We used to go *garbi* around it. No I didn't do garbi. I only watched." This puzzled the family greatly. From Rajkot, Rajul went to Wankaner and Mr. V. J. Shah and his daughter (Rajul's aunt), Sudha, began to ask her about Junagadh. The conversation between Sudha and Rajul is quoted here exactly as it happened:

Sudha: Rajul, you say that you have come from Junagadh. What was your name in Junagadh?

Rajul: My name was Gita.

Sudha: What was name of Gita's mother?

Rajul: I don't remember.

Sudha: What was Gita's house like?

Rajul: Gita's house was not as big as this one. That house had only two rooms and a kitchen.

Sudha: Was it like your Papa's house in Keshod?

Rajul: No. Not like Papa's house in Keshod. Papa's house has only one room and one kitchen.

Rajul was very fond of *pedas*. Once she commented, "Here we make white pedas but in Junagadh we made yellow ones. We arranged them in a cupboard."

As Shahs are Jains, they eat their supper before the sun sets. One day, Rajul casually remarked, "Grandmother, we eat very early here. In Junagadh we used to eat late, at arti time."

To the query as to what they ate from, Rajul replied, "In our house there was only one steel *thali*. My Papa ate from the steel thali, the rest of us ate from brass thalis." On and off, Rajul used to say, "Here we take milk in a small saucepan. In Junagadh we took milk in a big pot and we poured some of the cream on top into a small saucepan and from the milk in the big pot we made pedas." Most of these statements came spontaneously from her, almost casually. Even when questioned again, Rajul's answers were always the same. If someone pestered her with repeated questions, she would say, "I have told you that truth. Why do you ask me again and again?"

In August 1965, Rajul and grandparents went to Songadh to visit Himat Bhai, the younger brother of Mr. V. J. Shah. It was there that some of her statements startled the family.

Himat Bhai asked Rajul, "Rajul, if we go to Junagadh, would you show us Gita's house?"

Rajul replied in the affirmative.

"Will you show us Gita's mother and father?"

"Yes, I will."

"Will you show us Gita?"

"How can I show you Gita? I am Gita."

Shahs being well-educated and religious, thought this could be a case of "past memory". They decided to investigate it.

However, there was one difficulty about making inquiries in Junagadh. Rajul did not remember the names of Gita's parents.

It is a Jain belief that a soul cannot exist without a physical body unless it has attained Nirvana. Rajul's parents, therefore, calculated the probable month of Gita's death as October 1959. That is the approximate time of Rajul's conception. Rajul's grandfather, Mr. V. J. Shah, took a chance and made enquiries in Junagadh.

There was a death recorded in the Municipal Register of a girl named Gita on October 28, 1959. Her father's name was Gokuldas Luhana. Her mother's name was given as Kanta Ben. Their address was Talao Street.

Since Rajul talked of pedas often, the Shahs assumed that Gokuldas would be a confectioner. In November 1965, Mr. and Mrs. V. J. Shah, along with their daughter Sudha, took Rajul to Junagadh. They were joined there by Himat Bhai and his wife from Songadh. They planned that they would carry out the preliminary investigations on their own. On getting sufficient evidence, they would take Rajul for identifying the places she had described.

Next morning, they went to search Talao Street. They had some difficulty in locating Gokuldas, because he had changed his residence. However, they came to a shop owned by the brother of Gokuldas. Gokuldas Thaker (Luhana) had a grain shop. Enquiries revealed that Gokuldas had a daughter named Gita, who died of measles at the age of two-and-a-half years. It may interest the readers to know that Rajul had told her parents that she had died of fever and that when she was gone, she became Rajul. It was confirmed that Gita had a very mild rash and high fever and that she died in the auspicious hours of dawn.

You may ask: Why should I bother about my previous birth?

The answer to this is significant.

Many children today carry the memory of their previous birth. Some of this memory is loaded with negativity. The parents get worried over their children's negative behaviour and, in the process, their behaviour and their children's behaviour becomes more negative and unbalanced. Their worry becomes huge if the child's behaviour is deviant. All negativity is bad. It should be dispelled, but in a positive way.

Here is a simple solution:

The Crystal Sight

The memory of the past life remains up to three or five years. Hence, we should treat the child with compassion and care. The negativity can be dissolved through Reiki, pranik healing, through physiotherapy and mantra jaap, or through a holy person's pure vibrations. If you treat the child with harshness, then the child might rebel and grow up to be a disgruntled person.

Mischief Mongers: The Mystery of Roaming Souls

Rare and strange phenomena have always intrigued humankind. These mysterious occurrences have often been dubbed as superstition, black magic and hallucination. And yet, none of these descriptions are totally accurate. As a child, I used to hear my mother say that beds in the attic of her ancestral home changed position without anyone ever touching them. Later, I sighted a manuscript written by my great grandfather describing the working of poltergeists in his attic. These descriptions were corroborated by my husband's grandmother, who once lived in the same place.

In 1970s, while writing a series of articles for a women's weekly, I met Prof. V. V. Akolkar of Pune. In his generosity, he gave me several of his research papers to use in my writings.

While going through those papers, two strange cases came to light. Both were of poltergeists. "Poltergeist" is a German word meaning a ghost who creates a disturbance. As these cases had evoked international interest, I produce them here as documentary facts.

> On 4 September, 1973, an unusual frightening thing happened in the house of a Sindhi family in Phaltan. The paper decoration around the Ganapati idol on the wall was seen smouldering by Devaki, a twelve-year old schoolgirl. As her parents were in Kalayan, she called her two sisters-in-laws to witness the phenomenon. In the evening, Devaki found the tablecloth under radio-set burning. On Thursday noon, a coir mattress emitted smoke.

> Since it was always Devaki who first sighted the burning, aspersions were cast on her. However, two hours later, when Devaki was in school, a pant and a shirt caught fire. That evening, smoke swirling out of a closed cupboard terrified the family and they removed all their clothing to a neighbour's place.

> Friday marked the climax. Yellow flames were sighted inside a closed almirah which had glass panes. A little later *jawar* bags caught fire in the presence of the younger sister-in-law. Dr. Karwa, a local physician, planted himself in the house. He witnessed the burning of a wet, soiled napkin used by Devaki.

> The family was bewildered. The frequency of incidents was increasing rapidly. The burning, which was originally confined to one room, now spread to other areas. Many theories were put forward. Was the family being haunted by an evil spirit? Was it an invisible trick? The news of the weird phenomenon brought in friends and relations. They stood guard to detect the mischief maker. But to no avail.

On Saturday morning, one of the beds caught fire, plunging the family into a miserable panic. Children were sleeping on that bed. Then worse followed. At 8.00 a.m., there was an explosive sound. A packet of groundnuts kept in kerosene tin was crackling. But the kerosene did not burn. This mystified everyone.

By now the family was so distressed that they sought help of a mantric. Incredibly, the spontaneous burning of objects stopped with his intervention. This phenomenon lasted from 4 September to 10 September 1973. It was witnessed by the Headmaster of Phaltan High School, the editor of a local paper, and the cloth merchant who owned the house.

Prof. V. V. Akolkar, on getting the news, rushed to Phaltan. He, along with a physical scientist, examined the house. There were no holes or leakages in the roof or walls through which fire could have been ignited by acid drops or matchsticks. The kerosene tin was examined by a Chemist. Dr. Joshi of Pune, an internationally renowned authority in Chemistry, ruled out the possibility of acid or phosphorous in the kerosene tin.

How did the phenomenon occur? How did it end with the mantric's recitation of *Devi Saptshadi*? How could the two black dolls given by mantric be so efficacious? Was it black magic or a paranormal occurrence? Prof. Akolkar dismisses the questions with a cryptic, "I have given you the facts."

While spontaneous burning is a rare happening, the movement of objects is not. Objects do mysteriously disappear from their places. But the frequency with which this happened with a family in Aurangabad was puzzling.

It was in September 1974 that the lady of the house found a wood apple (bel fruit) disappear from the table. As she urgently needed a wood apple to make chutney for her son, who was ailing, she bought another one from the market. But no sooner did she keep it on the table and turned to get the jaggery, the wood apple was gone. Subsequently, vegetables, wheat flour dough, and even milk kept inside the kitchen cupboard disappeared.

But a stranger thing was to follow. After two days, the lady of the house saw a pickle jar move along the wall for a distance of 11 feet. The moment she turned her back, the pickle jar turned upside down, splashing the pickle on the floor. Quickly, she picked up the jar in the hope of retrieving the pickle. But lo and behold! The lime pickle had disappeared in thin air.

By this time, the family was terribly upset and felt persecuted. They were relieved when the oldest son, aged 28, and his wife, aged 21, came to visit them. The oldest son, an employee in the Electricity Board, was amused when he saw a 70 kg wheat bag move for a distance of five feet. Marked by curiosity, he invited people to witness the phenomenon. Mr. Jagdhane, a local businessman, was one of them. He vouchsafes that the idli-sambhar he had kept in a vessel in the kitchen, planting his son as an investigator, disappeared the moment the boy raised his head to tell the audience that nothing was happening.

The harassed family ultimately brought in a mantric. The family was to install an idol of Mahalaxmi, but now wondered whether that would be suitable. The mantric permitted the family to have Mahalaxmi puja as scheduled. He also performed his rituals. Thereafter, the phenomenon stopped.

Prof. Parandandiwad, Head of the Chemistry Department, Government College, Aurangabad, and Dr. Bhurda, Professor of Psychology, again of Government College, visited the family and investigated the matter. Later, Prof. V. V. Akolkar interviewed the troubled family and discussed the phenomenon at length. He also met the mantric. Like the Sindhi family at Phaltan, this Maharashtrian family, too, believed that it was an evil spell cast on them by an enemy, which only the power of mantras could dispel.

Several hundred cases of poltergeists have been reported and examined by various authorities. In Germany, a team of eight scientists (four physical scientists and four social scientists) of Freiburg University, of which Dr. Hans Bender was a well-known figure, had investigated the cases, and also filmed some of the phenomena. These Western scientists

are of the view that there is always a central figure involved in these cases. The unconscious mind of this figure propels the movement of objects; the propelling is done by the bio-energy released by the unconscious thought. Further, these scientists state that the central figures tend to have a neurotic personality — a point which is highly debatable, as according to psychology each one of us has neurotic tendencies.

Dr. William Roll of Psychical Research Foundation (Durham, North Carolina) along with Dr. Owen of Germany, studied the poltergeist cases from a physical angle. They have studied cases of falling stones and hitting objects. According to them, when the central figure is stationary, the objects move towards it and when the central figure is moving, the objects follow it from behind.

The opinion of the Indian scientists, however, is basically conditioned by the beliefs in reincarnation, possession by spirits, and the earth-bound troubled spirits. Their conclusions, therefore, are in favour of spirituous. The science of spirits is still in its infancy. But time is not far when many of the so-called mysteries will be unravelled and shall reckon with the truth of strange occurrences on this planet, which then may not seem strange at all.

The Crystal Wisdom

The dislodged or earth-bound souls can be avoided by wearing a talisman, or protection ring or bracelet. According to the Hindu belief, one should avoid crossroads in the dark, or certain trees or dark corners. Simple solution for your house is to light a lamp in dark corners or keep a crystal as it dispels darkness. Or just keep the shrine lamp burning all night. Recitation of a verse from a holy book or incantation of a mantra every day protects the house and its people from an evil eye and evil spirits.

Justice through Reincarnation

Dream, Reincarnation, and the Settlement of Karmic Debt!

Story of Dhanpal and Govindsinh

Here is an interesting story of reincarnation.

> Govindsinh lost his job once again — for the fourth time within five years. Govindsinh decided not to serve anyone again, if he could do something on his own. With this determination in mind, he was on the look-out for someone to finance his scheme to open a concern for manufacturing tools.
>
> Luckily for him, one morning he heard that Dhanpal, an old friend, had become rich overnight only a few days earlier. So he went to him with his plans, seeking finance to establish a small tools factory in partnership with his old friend.
>
> Dhanpal had no sisters or brothers. After the death of his father, a distant uncle got him married off and he was living with his mother, wife, and three children.
>
> About this time, Dhanpal's grandfather fell seriously ill and, for some reason, prior to his death, chose to name Dhanpal in his will as the legal heir to his movable and immovable properties. That was how Dhanpal became rich overnight.
>
> Dhanpal had never ever dreamed of coming by such a big fortune. He did not know what to do with it. And because Govindsinh happened to be a good friend, in dire need of help, Dhanpal readily agreed to his friend's proposal and promised to invest sixty thousand rupees in the factory which Govindsinh intended to start.
>
> At that time, Govindsinh was hit by the bug of greed and somehow an idea got into his head to cheat Dhanpal.
>
> With this deceitful thought filling his head, Govindsinh took various amounts from the simple minded Dhanpal on the pretext of purchasing machines and material, totalling to twenty thousand rupees, but never spent any money for that purpose. His intention was to swindle Dhanpal outright.
>
> As per his plans, one day Govindsinh proceeded to Sachin, a town near Surat, to search for a suitable site for the location

of the factory. He craftily explained to his friend Dhanpal that Sachin was a far more economical location because it was nearer to Bombay and situated on the main line. Thus, it would be feasible to establish business relationship with Maharashtra and at the same time cover the rich region of South Gujarat, too.

Govindsinh and Dhanpal proceeded to Sachin on the following day, for making payment and for preparing the necessary documents for the plot to be purchased by them. Dhanpal gave Govindsinh forty thousand rupees to carry to Sachin to make the payment there.

Now that the entire amount of sixty thousand rupees had come into his hands, Govindsinh carefully hid the amount in a safe place and took care not to divulge even to his wife anything in regard to the fraud which he intended to perpetrate.

On the next day, they both left for Sachin. There they met the agent of the land-owner and Govindsinh pursued the mock talks about the purchase.

Both returned to Surat to catch the fast down-train for home. Both managed to squeeze into a compartment just as the train was leaving and they had to stand on the brink of the gangway, keeping the door of their compartment open.

In the moving train, Dhanpal put a number of questions to Govindsinh on diverse matters connected with the building and running of their factory. Time passed on in this manner, when, giving a shocking twist to their talks, Govindsinh blurted out, "Well, friend! The truth of the matter is, our plans will now take a little more time to take shape. Because the amount of rupees forty thousand which you had entrusted to my care, was lost yesterday and . . ."

"Ah! You rascal, you have ruined me!" exclaimed the agitated Dhanpal. As his hold on the handlebar of the door got loosened in that disturbed mental state and as there were heavy jerks since the train was passing the bridge over the river Narmada near Broach station, Dhanpal somehow lost his balance and was thrown out of the train.

Govindsinh didn't expect such a thing to happen; he didn't desire so either. With genuine concern, therefore, he instantly rushed inside the main compartment and pulled the alarm chain to stop the train.

At the railway station, Govindsinh made a detailed report. He also informed the police that Dhanpal carried with him a bag containing rupees forty thousand in cash.

Govindsinh returned to his home on the second day. Proceeding straight to Dhanpal's house, he narrated to Gita Devi, his friend's wife, the whole incident, with a great show of sorrow.

On the third night, the departed Dhanpal appeared in Govindsinh's dream and said threateningly, "My inner-self tells me that you have wilfully defrauded me, accelerated my death, and deprived my wife and children the care and comforts which they could have enjoyed with my inherited wealth. Take heed, clearly, you shall pine and pay for your cold blooded betrayal."

This threatening dream momentarily shook Govindsinh. But in the hardened heart, he didn't take long to brush it off from memory as a mere hallucination.

Govindsinh made it a point to visit the house of the late Dhanpal with an increased frequency and assisted Gita Devi in various matters, especially those requiring outdoor work. In this manner, he covered up and cleared all possible doubts in the minds of people regarding his innocence, especially with regard to the death of Dhanpal.

With the passage of time, Govindsinh's wife gave birth to a charming baby boy and it was another event for the couple to be happy about. After the birth of a son, Govindsinh's income also began to increase.

Days passed on into weeks; the weeks into months; the months into years and soon the young child was two years old. He was a jovial little child of attractive features and everyone liked and loved him.

One morning, as Govindsinh was playing with his little son, as he very often did, strangely enough the young fellow gave his father stiff slap on the face. Govindsinh naturally took it for a childish prank and even enjoyed it. But when he looked at his son, he was puzzled to observe his infant son's face red with rage and his lips twitching as if to say something. Soon, the boy began to shiver and Govindsinh slowly laid him on a bed in the room and watched him nervously. He did not know what had happened to his son or what might follow.

Govindsinh was greatly alarmed when once his son said in a condemning voice, "You acted very lowly for gaining money."

Govindsinh's memory went back to his dream on the third day of Dhanpal's accidental death. Inwardly, he began to fear, lest that earlier threat might come to pass.

On some later occasions, when his son began to speak in that enigmatical state of transportation to his past, Govindsinh used to silence the boy with severe admonitions.

One day, my friend Swami Sri Snehanandji, for whom both Govindsinh and the late Dhanpal had very deep respect, went to the house of Govindsinh as he did every year. Govindsinh's wife informed Swamiji of her son's unusual behaviour. She told him that her son often addressed her as "sister" and said, "You perhaps now know that your husband is a cheat. He has completely ruined me and, as a result, my wife and children have perforce to face avoidable privations."

She said that her husband relentlessly beat his son often. The boy, she added, feared his dad. She requested Swamiji to go through all the details and tell her what he felt might be behind it all.

"Late Dhanpal has himself reincarnated here to avenge the possible wrong suffered by him in the hands of Govindsinh," advised Swamiji.

On hearing this, the young boy became normal and the Swamiji was at once convinced that it was indeed a case of a reincarnated soul come into that family to settle the injustice meted out to it.

Govindsinh agreed to repay the amount he that taken from Dhanpal by cheating. He didn't have the entire amount in his possession right then and, therefore, begged for grace of time. He promised to repay the entire amount within three months.

Swamiji sent one of his disciples to go and pay the amount to Gita Devi. He instructed his disciple to pose as a debtor of the late grandfather of her late husband. When the final instalment was paid, with happy expressions lit over his face, Govindsinh's son loudly remarked, "Well, chum, I am glad to note that, after all, goodness did prevail in you, though only through the timely intercession of our venerable Swamiji. I forgive you from the core of my heart. May God bless you."

To our sad surprise, however, few days later, the little boy passed away as if he was a bill collector who comes, collects his dues, and goes off.

Crystal Wisdom

Live a life of honesty and purity.

Occult Powers of Yogis

I am grateful to Late Swami Krishnanandji of Bhadran for sharing the story in the year 1962, a few years after the incident had happened.

Around this time, Swamiji was helping Dr. Ian Stevenson of Virginia University in investigating the cases of reincarnation. Swamiji was very keen to find the connection between this life and the previous births. At a later stage he gave it up, because His permutation and combinations of deeds and actions, and their repercussions are beyond the human mind. In other words, those on the path find this as a futile exercise, because in the due course of time they are blessed by glimpses of their previous births.

To a lay person, this is interesting as it brings solace that you receive what you give; you reap what you sow.

The above incident is quoted from Swamiji's book Reminiscences, Crystal Wisdom.

Mukundbhai Patel worked as a professor of Economics at Bhadran College from 1966 to 1986. During this time, he came in contact with Swami Krishnanadji of Bhadran. Subsequently, Mukundbhai shifted to Atlanta, USA.

This is Mukundbhai's story:

One day, my grandfather, who lived in Bhadran, said, "Swamiji gets up at 2.30 a.m." As a young, rational being, I found this mysterious. Why should anybody get up at 2.30 a.m.? To verify, I decided to find out for myself. Next day, at 2.30 a.m. I walked into the ashram. Swamiji was up and already in meditation pose.

"Why have you come at such an early hour?" Swamiji asked.

"Just like that," I replied, hiding my real intention of finding out the truth about him.

But my curiosity was not satisfied. A few days later, I set the alarm for 2 a.m. and went to Swamiji's ashram at around 2.15 a.m. Swamiji was already up. As I stood outside the ashram, Swamiji asked from inside his meditation room, "Mukundbhai, so you have come!" I had not yet stepped in, but still Swamiji knew exactly who I was!

Much later, I came to know from another devotee, Prafulbhai Bakshi, about Swamiji's business at that hour of 2.30 a.m. Swamiji received requests or questions from his very close devotees and answered them telepathically between 2.30 and 3 a.m.

Once Swamiji was ill. He was hospitalized at a Baroda (now Vadodara) Hospital. I was attending to him. Swamiji said, "Mukundbhai, today do not touch my body." I was puzzled, as much as hurt. Why did Swamiji say, "Do not touch my body"? I had taken my bath and I was administering him his medicines, etc. All of sudden, this strange command from Swamiji was puzzling. Swamiji was a quick face-reader. He immediately understood my feelings.

"If you touch my body, I will find it difficult to get back into it," he said.

Swamiji was going on his "ether" travel. Where he was going, was unknown. Maybe to a higher sphere of the Universe, maybe he was answering a distress call.

It is a well-known and a recorded fact that Swami Ramakrishna Paramhans, the nineteenth century Indian saint made famous by his disciple Swami Vivekanand, had left his body for six months. He had given orders to his closest disciple, who was looking after his physical body, not to allow anyone to come inside his room. It is reported that Swami Ramakrishna's ether travel was on a "higher sphere".

One of the devotees of Swami Krishnanandji, by the name of Surendrabhai Trivedi, was in Houston. He had suffered an attack of paralysis. The doctors in USA treated him for several months, but without much success. His recovery seemed unlikely. He sent a message to Swamiji. One night, he felt Swamiji's presence in a dream. Swamiji's head was on his shoulder. "Come to India, come to Bhadran. You will be all right."

Surendrabhai travelled to Bhadran. He could not walk due to paralysis. Swamiji called me and said, "Take him to your house and look after him well." I took him home. Bhadran, with population of 8,000 people, had no lodge or hotel. Swamiji had a look at him and said, "Your problem is in your mouth, not in your legs. Please tell the USA doctors to examine your mouth." Back in USA, at Houston, Surendrabhai went through a check-up. He told the doctors about his "mouth". Doctors detected severe case of pyorrhoea. The poison had travelled to his legs. After the treatment of pyorrhoea, Surendrabhai became totally fit.

10

Mystical experiences

William Gibb:
A Sindhi knowingly or unknowingly is a mystic. This is true. Mysticism is a tradition with Sindhis. Mystical experiences were common in Sindh during my mother's time.

Hafz, the Sufi:
"For the enigma to resolve,
None ever knew nor yet shall know."

Dr. H. M. Gurbaxani:
When the body and mind in a state of trance become dead to all external impressions, the mystic is able, by means of this new faculty of perception, to experience vision and auditions.

    Mystics can see the future as the past. But they resist it. Their goal is to merge with the Super Conscious. Vision and auditions are incidental to mysticism.

Blake:
Each grain of sand
Every stone on the land
Each rock and each hill,
Each fountain and rill
Each herb and each tree
Mountain, hill, earth and sea
Cloud, meteor and star
Are men seem afar

Rumi:
I died from mineral and became the plant
I died from the plant and became the animal
I died from the animal and became the man
Why should I fear that in dying I become less?
Yet again shall I die from Man
That I may become an Angel.

Sources

Baldock, John, *Essence of Rumi*
Batra, Dr. Arjun, *Reiki Seminar Papers*
Dhyana, *Sri Aurobindo and The Mother*
Huffins, Launa, *Bridge of Light*
Krishnanand (Bhadran), Swami, *Reminiscences*
Maharishi, Yogiraj Vethathiri, *Journey of Consciousness*
Nahn, Nich Tinh, *Meditation*
Pritam, *Voice from Beyond*
Rasha, *Oneness*
Reiki *Questions & Answers*
Sha, Master Zhi Gang, *Soul Healing Miracles*
Umrigar, Nan, *Sounds of Silence*
Vasudev, Sadhguru, Inner Engineering
Vaswani, T. L., Ecstasy and Experiences
Vaswani, T. L., *Thus Have I Learnt*
Vivekananda, Swami, *Patanjali's Yoga Sutra*
The Yoga Sutras of Patanjali (Translation)